The Social Mission of Waldorf Education

Independent, Privately Funded, and Accessible to All

by

Gary Lamb

AWSNA

Printed with support from the Waldorf Curriculum Fund

Published by:

The Association of Waldorf Schools of North America
3911 Bannister Road
Fair Oaks, CA 95628

Title: The Social Mission of Waldorf Education
Independent, Privately Funded, and Accessible to All

Author: Gary Lamb
Editor: David Mitchell
Cover: Hallie Wootan
Proofreader: Ann Erwin
© AWSNA , 2004
ISBN: 1-888365-60-9

Curriculum Series

The Publications Committee of AWSNA is pleased to bring forward this publication as part of our *Curriculum Series*. The thoughts and ideas represented herein are solely those of the author and does not necessarily represent any implied criteria set by AWSNA. It is our intention to stimulate as much writing and thinking as possible about Waldorf Education, including diverse views. Please contact us with feedback on this publication as well as requests for future work.

David S. Mitchell
For The Publications Committee
AWSNA

TABLE OF CONTENTS

PART III

The Future of Waldorf Education

Acknowledgements

The author wishes to acknowledge and thank the following people and organizations for their help and support in making this book a reality. First of all, thanks to Emily Hassell Aguilar, Ame Kane-Barkely, and Jennie Neu-Duncan for transforming my handwritten notes into a typed manuscript. I was also fortunate to have a large number of colleagues who graciously read through numerous drafts and offered their editorial comments. These include Candace Bachrach, Jean Brousseau, James Marshall Knight, Jan Kibler, Joel Kobran, Patrice Maynard, Ronald Milito, Robert Monsen, Sophia Christina Murphy, Carolyn Polikarpus, John Root, Sr., Mary Roscoe, and Sherry Wildfeuer. Thanks also goes to Judith Kiely and Judith Soleil at the Rudolf Steiner Library in Harlemville, New York, for helping me find the pertinent reference material. An finally it is important to acknowledge that this book could not have been written without financial support, and I was fortunate to have received assistance from numerous sources, including: Foundation for Rudolf Steiner Books, Inc., Joseph and Diane Haley, Hawthorne Valley School, Rudolf Steiner Foundation, Waldorf Schools Fund, AWSNA Publications and Waldorf Educational Foundation. May this book be worthy of everyone's efforts and support.

– Gary Lamb
Ghent, NY
October 2004

PART I

THE THREEFOLD SOCIAL ORGANISM AND THE FOUNDING OF THE FIRST WALDORF SCHOOL

Introduction

Independent Waldorf schools require the good will and support of a broad range of people in order to flourish. The intent of this book is to provide facts and insights that will be of help to such supporters of the Waldorf movement, including teachers, teachers-in-training, staff, parents and their families, board members, volunteers, and donors. Waldorf teaching methods and the spiritual-scientific worldview, Anthroposophy, developed by Rudolf Steiner will be presented here only so far as to enable the reader to gain insight into the movement's history and social mission. A modern perspective of this mission will be given in the context of current United States educational reform efforts. The focus herein will be on the economic, political, and cultural challenges Waldorf education must address if it is to thrive in the twenty-first century.

Those making initial inquiries about Waldorf education may also discover much in this book that can be helpful. No prior knowledge of Anthroposophy is needed for appreciating or understanding the main thoughts expressed here, only a mind open to ideas that are not yet fully a part of the mainstream. People from countries other than the United States may find this exposition useful since education reform in the United States is in the forefront of what is similarly taking place in every modern industrial nation, and Waldorf education is now a worldwide movement with over a thousand schools and initiatives in diverse cultures.

This exploration into the social mission of Waldorf education will provide unique insights into the exceptional figure of Rudolf Steiner (1861–1925), the founder of the Waldorf school movement. Steiner had an innate capacity to perceive the spiritual reality underlying the physical world. He set himself the task of researching the supersensible world in a manner that is as scientifically rigorous as the one used in natural scientific research. He employed the results of his research in practical fields for the benefit of humanity in response to many requests for assistance and direction. He took the position that since there is a spiritual reality permeating earthly life, it can only benefit humanity at this point in human evolution if this reality is investigated and the results of these investigations are put to practical use in an ethical and effective manner. The fruits of Steiner's efforts have shown positive results not only in the education of so-called normal children but also in the education of children with special needs, as well as in the fields of natural science, medicine, agriculture, art, religious renewal, and architecture.

Readers will gain insight into the tremendous effort it takes to implement spiritual ideals in practical endeavors in our present age of materialism. Institutions and organizational forms are a reflection of the worldview out of which they are conceived and developed. Because Waldorf education is rooted in a spiritual-scientific worldview, it employs teaching methods and administrative forms that are often quite different from what is usually found in government-run public education, which is based on materialism and the apparent need to support accelerated economic growth.

There is another potential benefit from reading such a work for individuals who are studying Anthroposophy and threefold social ideas. It increases the possibility of developing social sensibilities that can be an aid in knowing what to do now in the twenty-first century and having the courage to follow through with what they know to be right. Simply repeating what Steiner said and imitating what he did decades ago serves no good purpose in relation to the issues facing Waldorf schools today. However, to the person who dismisses as irrelevant the quest to understand what Steiner did and why, suggesting that a more important question is: "What would Rudolf Steiner do today?" one must reply: "The essential question is what *you* will do!" And there is no better way to prepare oneself for the mighty challenges that come with striving for an ideal than to start with knowing the truth about past and present events. Developing the courage and strength needed to accomplish great deeds begins with a willingness to face the unvarnished truth, however much discomfort one may experience in the process.

The purpose of Waldorf education is to help young people begin the life-long task of self-education. It is not to teach Anthroposophy. Anthroposophy can, however, provide a perpetual source of knowledge and a practical method of self-development. From the perspective of Anthroposophy, each person consists of body, soul, and spirit, and each child descends to earthly life out of the heavenly world with intentions and latent capacities that have been developed through experiences in the spiritual world and in previous earthly lives. Not only as individuals but also as participants in the rising generation do they carry tasks into life related to personal destiny and the goals of human evolution. Indeed, each child and each generation are seen as bringing messages and impulses of social renewal from the spiritual world.

Taking this perspective as a given, the key to individual and social progress is that each generation of children should be able to develop its inherent capacities to the maximum, work on its preordained tasks, and release rejuvenating spiritual forces into social life. Thus teachers and the field of education as a whole have a pivotal role to play in social progress. This necessitates that teachers continually work to develop a greater and greater sensitivity for both the unique capacities and intentions of each child in their charge and the important traits of the generation of which they are a part. Consequently, the active Waldorf teacher strives to take into consideration not only physical heredity and environmental influences but also the spiritual heritage of the child and of humanity as a whole. Although each child carries within him or her an eternal core with unique predilections, all modern people go through similar developmental stages that are subject to laws and forces both physical and soul-spiritual. Consequently, there are common teaching methods and a sequence of learning experiences incorporated into the curriculum of all Waldorf schools.

Freedom from outer constraints is essential for Waldorf teachers and schools. If teachers and schools are continually subjected to external regulations, goals, standards, and assessments generated by political and economic agencies located outside the field of education, the intimacy of the all-important student-teacher relationship is undermined. This book will reveal how big business and the federal government have systematically striven for uniform educational goals and standards over the last twenty-five years in the United States, and that this activity presents a grave threat to the very existence of Waldorf education, which by its very nature must remain independent. Everything connected to the school, including its administration, is an extension of the dynamic interaction between teachers and students. This makes the necessity of working closely with the parents who entrust their children to the teachers and school essential and provides significant opportunities and challenges.

Another challenge facing Waldorf education that will be covered here is the controversial effort by a growing number of people to separate it from its spiritual source, Anthroposophy, and from its founder, Rudolf Steiner. The goal is to create what are sometimes in the United States called *second generation Waldorf schools,* in which teachers use aspects of Waldorf teaching methods and curricula, without developing a relation to Anthroposophy. Such efforts are due to the perceived success of the independent Waldorf school movement worldwide and the desire of certain people to make Waldorf education available to a larger number of children as quickly as possible, through so-called Waldorf-inspired public schools.[1] This controversy and many other problems that the Waldorf schools face arise out of the fact that there is too little money available for independent Waldorf schools and families who want to send their children to them. Therefore, an important part of this work will focus on the question of how to finance Waldorf education.

Attempts to incorporate Waldorf education into the public school system have generated attacks on Anthroposophy and Rudolf Steiner, portraying them both as elitist and racially prejudiced.[2] It will be shown that, to the contrary, it is precisely through implementing Steiner's pedagogical and social ideas that humanity has the greatest possibility of addressing the most significant social issues of our time: economic exploitation, political oppression and imperialism, and cultural intolerance, including racism and nationalism.

The Waldorf school movement evolved out of a broad social movement based on Steiner's ideas, sometimes called the movement for a threefold social organism or a threefold social order. This is really the womb out of which Waldorf education emerged.

꙼

CHAPTER 1

THE THREEFOLD NATURE OF SOCIAL LIFE

The movement for the threefold social [organism] strives for the complete disassociation of the educational system from government and industry.[3]

—Rudolf Steiner

In 1917, Otto von Lerchenfeld, a member of the Bavarian State Council in Germany was in despair over the World War that was taking place. He decided to ask Rudolf Steiner for his opinion on what it would take to restore order and create a lasting peace. Von Lerchenfeld was familiar with Anthroposophy and was hoping some new ideas could come from this all-encompassing spiritual perspective. He was not disappointed. Over a three-week period Steiner laid out for von Lerchenfeld his thoughts on the World War and what needed to be done to avoid further violence and social upheaval. Steiner maintained that both capitalism and socialism were based on outdated ideas that did not take into consideration a complete view of reality. Neither capitalism, based on self-interested behavior and the impersonal market, nor socialism, which thwarts individual creativity and efficiency, could provide the foundation for a lasting peace.

Steiner described in detail to von Lerchenfeld how there are three primary aspects inherent in social life: the economy, the political-legal or rights life, and spiritual-cultural life. Each of these spheres or realms, if rightly organized, should have its own basis, dynamics, scope of action, function, and even administration. All three realms should be viewed as being of equal importance to the others, and each realm relates to the others in specific ways. Steiner maintained that one of the primary causes of modern social upheavals is the chaotic intermingling of the three realms in what he called the *unitary state*. The most significant modern-day example of one sphere inappropriately intruding upon another is that of big business using economic power to influence the creation of laws and regulations to suit its purposes without proper regard for human rights or the environment. Another example, which will be covered in some depth later, is the combined effort of big business and the state to form and control education, a cultural matter, to benefit their interests.

The proper scope of action for economic life is the production, distribution, and consumption of goods and services. A healthy economy requires individual initiative, efficiency, and technical expertise. Steiner maintained that economic decisions should no longer be left to unregulated market forces, as in capitalism, nor given over to the state, as in socialism, but should be decided in economic associations that include actual participants in the economy from all three sectors: production, distribution, and consumption. He maintained that we are at the point in human evolution when the economy must be taken consciously in hand by those active in it and who operate out of social needs or concern for others rather than self-interest. This altruistic approach can be called *brotherhood* or human fellowship, which is based on cooperation and collaboration.

The activity of the political or legal sphere should be limited to recognizing and upholding human rights, including those related to personal safety and security and the protection of the environment. Here the principle of *equality* should prevail in the decision-making processes. The scope of action of a political state, based on democracy[4] and majority rule, should be limited to those decisions that every competent adult is capable of understanding and acting upon. This would preclude the political state from making business decisions or decisions that involve personal views, such as religious beliefs, nutritional preferences, and medical and educational choices. In a healthy social life individuals and organizations directing economic and cultural activities would take democratically determined rights as a given. Quite the reverse perspective has become the norm in modern life—for instance, when the political state takes economic interests as a given when creating laws. The ultimate modern-day manifestation of this type of reversal is exemplified by the World Trade Organization's power to overrule existing laws of the world's nation-states and their inherent political communities, and even to influence or stop the creation of new legislation.

The spiritual-cultural realm includes everything connected with education and human development, including science, art, and religion. This realm is intimately related to the unique nature of each individual person and what is commonly called private life. Consequently, the fundamental basis for a spiritual-cultural sphere can only be individual *freedom*. According to Steiner, an independent cultural life would continually supply the other spheres with creative forces of spiritual renewal, something it cannot do if it is subject to the dictates of business and political interests wanting to perpetuate existing arrangements. The most significant value-forming area of spiritual-cultural life is the entire field of education, which from a threefold perspective should be independent of political and economic influences in the same way, as is commonly acknowledged, that religion should be free from their control.

The basis of each of the three spheres—spiritual-cultural, political, and economic—is revealed by the slogan of the French revolution: *Freedom, Equality,* and *Brotherhood.* In such a threefold arrangement, the unity of the social organism comes about through each individual, since everyone lives in all three spheres at any given moment. It also can come about by representatives from each of the three spheres meeting to discuss and reach agreements on common concerns, such as education, in a similar manner to the way heads of state meet, make agreements, sign treaties, and so on.[5]

Following Steiner's explanation of the threefold nature of social life to von Lerchenfeld, there were numerous efforts by enthusiasts to introduce these ideas to the ruling powers of Europe at the end of World War I. Steiner wrote a memorandum about threefolding that was circulated to significant political figures. Petitions drawn up in support of the social ideas outlined by Steiner were displayed in large advertisements in the major European newspapers. Steiner also lectured widely to all types of audiences, ranging from a few patrons of local smoke-filled taverns to audiences of several thousand union workers. In 1919, Steiner published the book *Towards Social Renewal*, which became a best-seller in Germany. It was soon translated into English and favorably reviewed in the *New York Times* newspaper. Unfortunately, after about three years following the war, when people were at least open to considering new social ideas, the old thought forms prevailed, and attempts to gain widespread recognition for the threefold nature of social life ceased. Steiner and his supporters then focused their efforts on smaller projects such as The Coming Day holding company in Germany, the Futurum enterprise in Switzerland, the Waldorf School in Stuttgart, efforts to start a World School Association, the refounding of the Anthroposophical Society, and lecturing to economists.[6] In principle, Steiner never gave up trying to harmonize the initiatives he was responsible for with the threefold nature of social life. He adjusted his strategy on how, when, and where to introduce these ideas according to the human capabilities of those involved, and the opportunities and challenges that presented themselves in outer life.

Since the principal dynamics of a threefold social organism are integrated and have to do with the arrangement of the whole of social life, it is not possible for a solitary organization to manifest all the principles of a threefold social organism or to be threefolded. Only when, in a given geographic region, enough individuals and organizations working in all three realms of life —cultural, political, and economic — harmonize their actions in line with threefold principles, will it be possible to have the requisite cooperation necessary to establish the beginnings of a threefold social organism. Although one can observe numerous worthy initiatives and movements taking place now, the necessary convergence of separate efforts has not developed to the point that a threefold organism can emerge.

This does not mean, however, that individuals and organizations should not try to gain an understanding of threefold principles and harmonize their actions as far as possible with them. Indeed, human evolution depends upon such efforts; all great social movements begin with individual actions.

We are at a stage of development when many social movements have matured to a significant degree but often are working separately. These movements include community supported agriculture, organic foods, community land trusts, sustainable communities, living wage, socially responsible investing and philanthropy, fair trade, intentional communities, alternative medicine, Waldorf education, biodynamic agriculture, permaculture,[7] and so on. It is entirely possible that a tremendous leap forward, a spiritual counterforce to materialistic tendencies, could take place if activists from the various movements would consciously strive to understand Steiner's social thoughts and use them to develop common ideals and strategies.

Steiner was one of the first persons to elaborate the threefold nature of modern social life to any significant degree. However, social life is now commonly portrayed as consisting of three main sectors. Some of the more recent proponents of a three-sector society are former Democratic New Jersey Senator Bill Bradley, David Korten, the anti-globalist author and activist, and the socialist-lean-ing professors and authors from the Massachusetts Institute of Technology, Jean L. Cohen and Andrew Arato. These thinkers subscribe to the same basic modern threefold characterization consisting of a market economy, political government, and civil society. Thus far, however, their characterizations have little correlation to Steiner's perspective in theory or practical application even though there may be a similar striving for social improvement. The fact that a threefold characterization of society has become commonplace has, to a certain degree, vindicated Steiner's visionary insights into social life.[8]

CHAPTER 2

THE FOUNDING OF THE
FIRST WALDORF SCHOOL: IDEALS,
CHALLENGES, AND COMPROMISES

In the end, the Waldorf School movement is connected to the threefold movement. The Waldorf School movement is conceivable only within a free spiritual life.[9]

Today I would like to speak to you about the Waldorf School, founded by our friend Mr. Molt. You know from the announcements distributed about this school that our intention is to take a first step along the path we would want the cultural life of the Threefold Social Organism to take. In establishing the Waldorf School, Mr. Molt has, to a large extent, felt motivated to do something to further the development of inner spirituality. He hopes to do something that will point the way for the present and future social tasks of the Threefold Social Organism.[10]

– Rudolf Steiner

In 1919, Emil Molt was the esteemed company director and a shareholder in the Waldorf Astoria Cigarette Factory in Stuttgart, Germany, although he did not own sufficient stock to have controlling interest. Molt was held in such high regard by his workers that they called him "father." Similarly, Molt's paternal concern for his workers went far beyond the life of the factory. Once, for example, when he heard of a worker who was suffering from an illness due to a lack of proper nourishment, Molt bought his family a cow to provide milk.

In addition to his concern for the well-being of his workers, Molt had a deep appreciation for Rudolf Steiner's social ideas and the importance of education as a social force. He had been particularly inspired by Steiner's pamphlet "Education of the Child in the Light of Anthroposophy,"[11] which was published in 1907 long before there was any school initiative. The pedagogical and social ideals expressed there by Steiner kindled an inner flame in Molt that would blaze forth years later when outer destiny provided the opportunity to start a children's school. Molt ascribed the terrible events of WW I to a failure in education, and after the war he established an educational program for his workers that included a wide variety of topics, such as foreign languages, painting, history, geography, and current events. Although the workers were appreciative of the adult education courses, attendance dwindled over time because they found it difficult to keep up the classes after a hard day's work, and their minds had fallen out of the habit of learning about new things. Molt described that, following the termination of the adult classes,

[I] became absorbed by the idea of providing for children what was no longer possible in later years, and of opening the door to education for all children, regardless of their parents' income.

This idea became extremely pertinent after a conversation I had with one of my factory workers. I had been told that his son was recommended for higher education by his teacher on the basis of his grades. I saw the pride and joy in the father's face, and experienced what it means for a worker if his child is given such an opportunity, with the possibility of improving his station in life. But I also experienced how this joy is dampened when funds are not available—when the father simply does not have the means to pay for tuition and school supplies. I felt the tragedy of the working class: to be held back by lack of money from sharing in the education of the richer middle class. I also had a sense of what it would mean for social progress if we could support a new educational endeavor within our factory.

I began to share some of these ideas with my employees. They were immediately delighted by the notion of their own school, mainly be-

cause of the experiences they had gained during their [adult] lessons [at the factory]. The enthusiasm spread.[12]

Thus destiny provided Molt with the opportunity to act out of both his deepest personal paternal feelings for his workers and what he considered the highest social ideals embodied in the movement for a threefold social organism. As already mentioned, several attempts had been made to introduce threefolding on a grand scale, and Molt was active in many of these. In the founding of a children's school he saw a new opportunity to "take a first step along the path we would want the cultural life of the Threefold Social Organism to take" and "to do something to further the development of inner spirituality."

The basis of cultural life in a threefold social organism is *freedom*. Molt and Steiner tried to permeate the school—its teaching methods, governance structure, and relations to the state—with this principle. There are four aspects to the principle of freedom, and Molt and Steiner attempted to address all of them in the founding of the first Waldorf School.

One is freedom from outer coercion and indoctrination. State compulsory school attendance and licensing of schools are examples of coercion. Standardized curricula and testing for students, and state teacher training requirements are examples of indoctrination techniques. Steiner and Molt did everything possible to create a school in which the teachers, parents, and students could operate with as little outside control as possible.

A second aspect has to do with the removal of soul obstacles and bodily hindrances that can prevent a person from acting freely. In keeping with this aspect of freedom, Waldorf teaching methods and curriculum can be seen as hygienic measures that help harmonize body movements and the major soul functions of thinking, feeling, and willing. An imbalance or overemphasis of any one of these soul functions can actually introduce inner obstacles to becoming a self-reliant human being. An example of this is the preoccupation of modern education with cultivating the intellectual or thinking capacities of the child while neglecting the proper development of the life of feeling and will. Waldorf education can also be viewed as therapeutic in the sense that to a limited degree a Waldorf education can counterbalance harmful influences that a child may be exposed to in other aspects of his or her life.

A third aspect has to do with the full development of latent capacities needed to carry out one's decisions. It has already been mentioned that one of the goals of a Waldorf teacher is to develop the ability to sense what capacities in the child are wanting to unfold rather than viewing the child in behavioristic terms as a being to be filled with what the existing state and the economy need in order to perpetuate themselves.

Finally, in modern life the full development of self-reliant, capable, and free individuals can be thwarted through economic dependency. Consequently, it is essential for a healthy social organism to provide for a fair distribution of wealth so that there is financial opportunity and freedom of choice in education for every person. The extraordinary efforts by Molt and Steiner to raise sufficient funds so that every family who wanted to send their children to the first Waldorf school could do so will be described in the next chapter.

In early 1919, Molt told Steiner that he was going to speak to local government officials about the possibility of starting a school. Shortly thereafter, he made the decision to ask Steiner formerly for his help and guidance. It was on April 23, 1919, after a lecture Steiner gave to the factory workers, titled "Proletarian Demands and How to Put Them into Practice,"[13] that Molt asked Steiner to take on the planning and leadership of the new school. Molt later said he considered this the true birth date of the school.[14] Steiner enthusiastically accepted the task.

An appropriate characterization of the facts would be to say that Emil Molt was the founder of the first Waldorf school and that Steiner was the founder of the Waldorf School Movement and the source of its pedagogical methods. Due to a blend of fiery idealism and practical skills that both Molt and Steiner exhibited, the new school opened on September 15, 1919, in a renovated Stuttgart restaurant purchased by Molt, less than five months after Steiner agreed to help. The school began with eight grades and 256 children.

Great deeds meet many obstacles, some foreseen and some not. Molt encountered the usual assortment of logistical challenges, but one that he did not foresee was opposition by the local priest. When the priest heard that parents from his diocese were intending to enroll their children in the new school at the Waldorf Astoria factory, he informed the families that any child who attended the school would not be allowed to receive communion. He assumed that all the children would be indoctrinated in Anthroposophy at the school. Two Catholic factory workers asked for a meeting with the priest to hear in detail his reasons for proclaiming such a harsh punishment for what they considered to be a joyous and positive opportunity for their children. The two workers asked Molt to join them for the meeting. It was clear from the start that the priest's main concern was the relation of the school to Anthroposophy, and he declared that the school would be sectarian. Molt was well prepared for such an opinion and addressed the priest's concerns with candor and truthfulness. He explained that the school would not be teaching Anthroposophy and that during religious instruction time every religious denomination would be represented by its own priests or ministers. By the end of the meeting the two employees were so emboldened by Molt's candid responses that they firmly told the priest, "We will send our children to the Waldorf School even if the Bishop denies them communion, and you can just go and tell him that."[15] There was no need for such rebellious action because the priest reversed his decision and all the Catholic children in his diocese were granted permission to attend the Waldorf School.

A major area of concern was the reaction by the local authorities to the school. It was only through the narrowest political window of opportunity that the Waldorf School was founded in 1919 following the collapse of the German government in 1918. Even so, certain compromises had to be made. The three most significant ones that Steiner worked out with the education department were:

1) The local Board of Education had to approve the school.
2) Each teacher had to demonstrate that he or she was academically and morally fit to teach.
3) Students in the Waldorf School had to achieve learning goals equivalent to the local public school by the end of the third, sixth, and eighth grades so they could transfer out of the Waldorf School if their families so wished.[16]

But in his negotiations with the officials Steiner was forthright regarding his long-term goals, as described by Erich Gabert's introduction to *Rudolf Steiner's Conferences with the Teachers of the Waldorf School in Stuttgart:*

Rudolf Steiner never left the Minister of Education in any doubt that he had no intention of retreating one step from the principle of complete independence from the state. Indeed he made this clear by calling it the Independent Waldorf School [Freie Waldorfschule]. But with the legal situation as it was there was no way of achieving this except with compromises.[17]

The fact that government officials recognized Steiner's and Molt's goal of maintaining independence from the state was later confirmed by an inspector who did an in-depth study of the school in 1926 for the State of Württemburg.

The School is called the Free Waldorf School. It is free in the sense that it is not bound by any State curriculum—free, too, in the sense that it is not supported financially either by the State or by the town of Stuttgart, but is dependent entirely upon its own resources.[18]

In a private address to the teachers before the opening of the school, Steiner explained his position regarding the compromises that he made with the State.

Compromises are necessary, as we have not yet reached the point where we can accomplish an absolutely free deed. The State will tell us how to teach and what results to aim for, and what the State prescribes will be bad. Its targets are the worst ones imaginable, yet it expects to get the best possible results. Today's politics work in the direction of regimentation, and it will go even further than this in its attempts to make people conform. Human beings will be treated like puppets on strings, and this will be regarded as progress in the extreme. Institutions like schools will be organized in the most arrogant and unsuitable manner. A foretaste of this can be seen in the example of the Russian Bolshevik schools that are the death of any real education. We shall have a hard fight, yet we have to perform this cultural deed.

Two opposite forces have to be harmonized in the course of our work. On the one hand, we must know what our ideals are, yet we must be flexible enough to adapt ourselves to things that are far removed from our ideals. The difficult task of harmonizing these two forces stands before each of you. And you will only achieve this if you engage all the forces of your personality into it. Each one of you will have to put your whole personality into it right from the start.[19]

At this point in the narrative, readers may think that it would be too harsh to characterize recent educational reform efforts of the United States government in such terms today. It will be shown later, however, that equally strong characterizations can be applied to the modern educational goals, standards, and assessments now being developed and implemented through the collaboration of big business and the federal and state governments.

۞

CHAPTER 3

OWNERSHIP, FINANCES, AND FUNDRAISING
IN THE EARLY YEARS

Since Emil Molt did not have controlling interest as a shareholder in the Waldorf Astoria Cigarette factory, he relied on the
faith and respect his colleagues had for him to persuade the factory
directors to fund the school. It would not be too far off to say that
Molt simply willed the school into being out of the strength of his
personality. He convinced the management council to go along
with the establishment of the school before he actually discussed it
with the other shareholders. Simply put, they were horrified by the
project, but they reluctantly went along with their esteemed director "in just the same way that a father is in agreement when his son
spends too much."[20]

The firm initially put aside the sum of 100,000 marks to help
launch the school. As this was not nearly enough to even purchase
the property required, Molt personally paid 450,000 marks for the
initial property purchase. Even though most people have the im-
pression that the Waldorf Astoria Cigarette Factory owned and established the school, it appears that the firm never actually owned
the school. The school property was initially registered in Molt's
own name, unbeknownst even to the teachers.[21]

In addition to the initial sum of 100,000 marks mentioned,
the firm agreed to pay the teachers' salaries for the first year, and
subsequently they covered the tuition costs for the workers' chil-

dren and other close relatives of the factory workers. Molt was put in the awkward position of being the teachers' employer and even determining their individual salaries for the first year. The situation created tensions between Molt and the teachers until the complex and confusing situation was cleared up with the help of Rudolf Steiner. (See previous endnote.) The school grew rapidly each year due to the increasing number of non-Waldorf Astoria families that wanted to send their children to the school. (See Illustration 1.) In the first year, 191 out of 256 students were children of parents or relations working for the factory. In the second year the student population grew to 420 with about half from Waldorf families and half from outside. For the next few years the number of factory children remained relatively constant while the number of children from outside families increased significantly. As the school became better known, parents from all walks of life wanted the opportunity to send their children to this unique and innovative school. The children came pouring in.

Illustration 1			
The Growth of the Independent Waldorf School 1919 –1924[22]			
School year	Students	Teachers	No. of Classes
1919-1920	256	12-14	8
1920-1921	420	19	11
1921-1922	540	30	15
1922-1923	640	37	19
1923-1924	687	39	21
1924-1925	784	47	23

While Rudolf Steiner was alive, the school adhered to the principle that no one would be turned away from the school for financial reasons. Families not closely connected to the factory paid tuition according to financial ability. But there never seemed to be enough money, and the school was under incredible financial strain right from the beginning. Steiner admitted that this enrollment policy was the main reason for the huge financial strain the school experienced each year. "It is one of our principles that we do not require every child to pay tuition. That is the reason for our difficulties, namely that we accept children who cannot pay tuition."[23]

Rudolf Steiner and Emil Molt produced a veritable whirlwind of fundraising ideas for the school. The following is a list of funding sources and initiatives relied upon or at least attempted during Steiner's time.

1. Direct payment from the Waldorf Astoria Cigarette Factory

This included a cash sum of 100,000 marks to help launch the school, employing the teachers, and paying their salaries the first year. Subsequently, they subsidized the tuition of the children of factory workers, in full or part, for approximately twenty years.

2. Tuition payments from families having no affiliation with the Waldorf Astoria Factory

Those with means paid the full tuition amount. Others paid less or none at all. "We simply must continue to uphold the principle of accepting children who cannot pay fees."[24]

3. The personal resources of Emil Molt

Molt contributed 450,000 marks to purchase the school property and continually paid for a variety of expenses, as his means allowed, for the rest of his life.

4. Membership in the Waldorf School Association

The Waldorf School Association was formed on May 19, 1920, toward the end of the first year of the school's existence. It was a local association based in Stuttgart that took on the responsibility of the finances and fundraising efforts for the school and to educate the public about the Waldorf educational approach. The share-holders of the factory were pleased at the possibility of extending the responsibility for the finances of the school and putting Molt's project at more of a distance. Initially, the voting membership consisted of seven people including Rudolf Steiner and Emil Molt. To encourage the continued cooperation and support of the factory, Max Mark, a Waldorf Astoria board member, was made the honorary chairman of the Association. Later a member each from the College of Teachers and from the school's administration became members with voting rights. Steiner had hoped that the Association would gain thousands of members over time and that millions of marks could be raised each year through dues and contributions. Although the Association did raise considerable funds, the amount was not what Steiner hoped for nor did it meet the needs of the school.[25]

5. Patrons or financial godparents

Wealthy members of the Waldorf School Association were asked to become financial godparents of one or more students whose families could pay only partial or no tuition.

6. Contributions from members of the Anthroposophical Society, wealthy school parents, and local supporters

In his travels, lecturing to the public and members of the Anthroposophical Society, Steiner took the opportunity to let people know about the progress of the school and the need for financial support. He was somewhat cautious in his solicitations because there were other projects in need of money, including the first Goetheanum, the center of the Anthroposophical Society in Dornach, Switzerland.[26]

7. The founding of The Coming Day, an association of businesses and educational and research organizations dedicated to the support of cultural endeavors

In 1920, enthusiasts regarding Steiner's threefold ideas, including Molt, set up a holding company called *The Coming Day* (Der Kommenden Tag). The initiators wanted to present to the world a practical model of the economic sphere providing significant financial support for cultural endeavors, including education, scientific research, and therapeutic work. From the other side, it was hoped that scientific research would have a rejuvenating effect on the businesses by providing the businesses with inventions, new products, and better methods of production, and that schools such as the Waldorf School would provide the enterprises with skilled and creative workers and entrepreneurs.

Economic endeavors included were: a grain mill, a dietary and cosmetic manufacturer, a farm and saw mill, a box factory, a hostelry, a press, a tool factory, a book bindery, a mop factory, a juice factory, an insurance company, and, for a period of time, the Waldorf Astoria Cigarette Factory. Cultural endeavors included a scientific research institute and the Waldorf School.

The Coming Day purchased property for the school and provided loan capital for building additions at a time when the school was rapidly expanding. The Coming Day experiment was short-lived due to a variety of factors, including a general economic downturn in Germany and a lack of understanding and appreciation for its social goals by people both within and outside the holding company. It divested itself of most of its enterprises by 1925 and after that operated in a significantly reduced fashion.[27]

8. Proceeds from inventions and new products

This was another source of income that Steiner was hoping would yield significant capital. Several businesses did eventually form but did not create a significant income stream for the school in Stuttgart. The Weleda pharmaceutical and body-care company was one company that in time became a sizeable international firm, but its profits go mainly to support the Anthroposophical Society.[28]

9. The founding of a World School Association

The next chapter is devoted to this effort by Steiner, which never came to fruition, of creating a worldwide fundraising organ for Waldorf education.

৬৬

CHAPTER 4

THE WORLD SCHOOL ASSOCIATION

I am convinced that nothing is more important for the social development of humanity than the foundation of such a world association of schools which would then awaken a real sense for a free cultural and spiritual life in the widest circles of people.[29]

We must rouse an idealism that is willing to put its money purse at the service of the ideals of mankind. Anthroposophically oriented spiritual science must take hold of practical life in its thinking. Its thinking must not merely live high up in the clouds but must penetrate right down into its money purse.[30]
– Rudolf Steiner

"Nothing more important for the social development of humanity" are indeed powerful words, considering Steiner's ideals and all the activities that he was engaged in up to the time of this statement in 1921, only four years before his death. It is not possible to understand the true mission of Waldorf education without taking into consideration Steiner's efforts to launch such a world-wide association, even though it never came into being. As mentioned already, Rudolf Steiner was ever on the lookout for ways to financially support not only the Waldorf School but also other anthroposophically related endeavors.

Steiner soon saw that in order for the many worthwhile endeavors to grow and new ones to emerge, a widespread effort to raise funds on an ongoing basis was urgently needed. Beginning in July 1920, and for nearly two years thereafter, he promoted the idea of a World School Association (*Weldschulverein* in German, also translated as World Fellowship of Schools). He saw the proposed international association having three main tasks:

1. To centralize the fundraising and disbursements of monetary gifts for anthroposophical causes.

Steiner thought a centralized fund would be helpful to overcome the fundraising competition that was beginning to occur amongst the various anthroposophical endeavors. He also hoped a centralized organization could establish broad-based support far beyond what each organization could do individually and locally. He explained this to the teachers at the Waldorf School on July 29, 1920.

My idea was to centralize the entire financial organization. We want a central financial organization so that all money donated for anthroposophical use will go to one central organization. . . . The intention was to have all the money we receive go into a unified central fund and then be distributed according to what is needed.[31]

2. To create new and immediate additional income streams for the Waldorf School in Stuttgart and for the completion of the first Goetheanum in Dornach, Switzerland.

Steiner saw the establishment of a World School Association as the most important social activity one could engage in at the time. He was hoping that a huge movement would spread rapidly over the whole world that could quickly raise funds for anthroposophical endeavors.

People ask how much money one needs for all this. One cannot say how much, because there never is an uppermost limit. . . . It will be possible to establish this World [School Association] . . . if the friends who are about to go to Norway or Sweden or Holland, or any other country—England, France, America, and so on—awaken in every human being whom they can reach the well- founded conviction that *there **has** to be a World [School Association]. It ought to go through the world like wildfire that a World [School Association] must arise to provide the material means for the spiritual culture that is intended here.*[32]

3. To influence public opinion by promoting the idea of educational and cultural freedom to the broader public.

Steiner felt it was essential to influence public opinion in order to create a climate in which laws could be introduced and supported that were in favor of independent schools. He wanted to counter the trend of ever-increasing government control over education. Knowing that the teachers of the Waldorf School had more than enough to do teaching and administering schools, he encouraged others to become active in the threefold movement. The two things he did encourage the teachers to do were to write and speak out of direct experience about their achievements in the school. In other words, let the world know what independent teachers and schools can accomplish.

Ultimately the Waldorf school movement has meaning only to the degree that it strives for cultural freedom. Steiner connected the idea of freedom from state control with raising the requisite money required to operate independent schools.

A movement can free itself from [the root causes of sectarianism] if it will stand up to the world, fully within the laws of the land, so that there can be no confusion with regard to the legal aspects. And this is what I had in mind with regard to the World School Movement. I wished to create the right mood for the introduction of laws which would grant freedom to found schools entirely out of the needs for educational renewal. Schools can never be rightly founded out of majority decisions. This is why they cannot be run by the state.[33]

I am convinced that nothing is more important for the social development of humanity than the foundation of such a world associa-

tion of schools which would then awaken a real sense for a free cultural and spiritual life in the widest circles of people. If such a feeling were to exist throughout the world, Waldorf schools would not have to be founded as isolated experiments that exist by the grace of the State, but the State would then be compelled, where free cultural life really founds schools, to recognize these schools on their own account, without having to make this or the other stipulation.[34]

[W]e need a really practical attitude. This is lacking if those who are enthused about the ideas of the Waldorf School do not develop an understanding for the necessity of spreading the idea that schools must become independent of the state—if they do not employ their forces to bring about the liberation of the schools from the state. If you do not have the courage to strive for the liberation of the schools from the state, the whole Waldorf School Movement is of no avail. For it has meaning only if this movement grows into a free spiritual life.

For all this, we need what I should like to call an international endeavor, an international endeavor that does not merely go out into the world spreading principles as to how schools are to be established. This will take care of itself if, above everything else, money is made available for such schools. We need a World School Association in all civilized countries in order to make available as quickly as possible the greatest amount of means. On the basis of these means, it will be possible to create the beginning of a free spiritual life. Therefore, try, wherever you go, to work for the understanding of the freedom of the spiritual life, not merely through all kinds of "idealistic" endeavors; but work for understanding which will bring it about that to the greatest possible extent money becomes available for the erection of independent schools and independent colleges in the world.[35]

Much to his distress, his contemporaries failed to grasp the vital importance of liberating education for the sake of human evolution and the necessity of having sufficient funds to work toward that ideal. The necessary conviction was not there to fire the will. By 1922, Steiner openly declared that his efforts to stimulate interest in a World School Association were a failure. It was a bitter admission for him to make because he was convinced that if the necessary conviction and will had lived strongly enough in the hearts of his listeners the money would have flowed in abundantly! At times Steiner expressed himself in terms of frustration and outright anger when referring to the failure of people to grasp what was at stake and what needed to be done.

When the attempt was made to accomplish the deed of founding the World School Association as our only means of expanding beyond Central Europe, this attempt failed. It was to have encompassed the entire civilized world. The attempt to rouse whatever belief people had that the educational system must change, which was what was being attempted in the World School Association, was a miserable fiasco. There is such a terrible feeling of being rebuffed when you appeal to the will. I do not say that I am appealing for money in this case. We are lacking in money, but we are lacking in will to a much greater extent. The interest that exists does not go very deep, otherwise it would extend to the right areas. . . .

I am trying to speak today in a way that awakens enthusiasm, so that people feel the spiritual blood trickling in their souls and a large number of people who realize this will commit themselves, so that public opinion is aroused. Actually, I must say that at any point in the last twenty years when I tried to speak a language that appealed to people's hearts not only in a theoretical sense but to the heart as an organ of will, what I felt, first in the Anthroposophical Society and later in other groups, always made me wonder, "Don't people have ears?" It seemed that people could not hear things that were supposed to move from words to action. The experience of the fiasco of the World School Association was enough to drive one to despair. . . .

In order to maintain the Waldorf School and establish additional schools, we need a growing public conviction that continuing in the sense of the old school system will lead only to forces of decline within humanity. This conviction is what we need. . . .

Please excuse me, but in a certain respect I really cannot avoid saying that I know many people will recognize the truth in what I have just said, but you only really acknowledge the truth of something by doing something about it! By doing something about it! . . . We must try to work for ideas and ideals so that an ever-growing number of people are imbued with them.

If all the money that people spend today on unnecessary associations could be directed into our channels, then . . . [our treasurer] would have to report that our reserve is so large that we have to try to invest it fruitfully.

I do not believe at all that the main thing for us today is our lack of money. What we are lacking is the will to assert ourselves in real life, to insist that the portion of spiritual life that we acknowledge as true be given its due in the world.

The will to convince everyone must be present in an ever-increasing number of people. In addition, the conviction must become widespread that for the salvation of humanity, it is necessary for something such as is present in embryonic form in the Waldorf School to keep on growing.

That is what I wanted to have said to the percentage of hearts in which the impulse of will is present. We can get very far if we only think about what it depends on: It depends on us using our will to really get public opinion to where it ought to be.[36]

It is interesting to note that even though he considered the creation of a World School Association to be so important for the proper growth of the Waldorf School Movement and the salvation of humanity, Steiner considered the effort to be a compromise in the way one should ideally go expanding independent school education.

So much about the planned World School Movement, an idea which in itself does not at all appeal to me. . . . All propaganda-making, all agitating is alien to me. I abhor these things. But if one's hands are tied and if there is no possibility to found free schools, one first has to create the right climate for ideas which may eventually lead to freedom in education. Compromises may well be justified in various instances, but we are living in times in which each compromise is likely to pull us still further into difficulties.[37]

࿔

CHAPTER 5

INDEPENDENCE AND SELF-ADMINISTRATION

Newcomers to Waldorf schools are often confused by the schools' administrative structures. Typically, there is no easily-seen authority figure directing the operations, no principal as is found in public schools, nor a headmaster or headmistress as found in traditional independent schools. Rather, the newcomers are confronted with titles and explanations of leadership positions and governance systems in terms of mandated committees, coordinators, facilitators, faculty chairs, and the college of teachers or teachers' council. Before giving a description of what Rudolf Steiner called a "republic of teachers," which is the basis for this unusual division of labor and of administrative functions, we will give the reasons for such an approach.

Below are five quotations by Rudolf Steiner from various written sources and lectures. They are given so the reader can grasp the context in which Steiner always spoke of school administration. While the material presented has redundancies, it also has subtleties and nuances that are helpful in understanding the full context and import of the principle of self-administration for an independent school. The repetition of certain thoughts expressed also shows that they are fundamental rather than isolated ideas. Steiner's indications regarding a teacher-run, self-administered school on a republican basis are meaningless unless they are understood in relation to the striving for educational freedom. Readers can gain considerable insight into the social mission of Waldorf education by meditatively contemplating the totality of these statements.

*The nature which spiritual [cultural] life has assumed requires that it constitute a fully autonomous member of the social organism. The administration of education, from which all culture develops, must be turned over to the educators. Economic and political considerations should be entirely excluded from this administration. Each teacher should arrange his or her time so that he can also be an administrator in his field. He should be just as much at home attending to administrative matters as he is in the classroom. No one should make decisions who is not directly engaged in the educational process. No parliament or congress, nor any individual who was perhaps **once** an educator is to have anything to say. What is experienced in the teaching process would then flow naturally into administration.[38]*

The threefold [organism] strives to realize an independent life of thought, especially in . . . everything relating to education and the manner of giving instruction, that is, the State shall no longer determine the matter and manner of teaching. Only those who are actually teachers, engaged in practical education, shall be its administrators. This means that from the lowest class . . . up to the highest grade of education, the teacher shall be independent of any political or economic authority as regards the subject or manner of his teaching. This is a natural consequence of a feeling for what is appropriate to the life of thought within the independent cultural body. The individual need only spend so much time in imparting instruction as will leave him leisure to collaborate in the work of education as a whole and the sphere of spiritual and cultural life.[39]

[T]he movement for the threefold social [organism] strives for the complete dissociation of the educational system from government and industry. The place and function of educators within society should depend solely upon the authority of those engaged in this activity. The administration of the educational institutions, the organization of courses of instruction and their goals should be entirely in the hands of persons who themselves are simultaneously either teaching or otherwise productively engaged in cultural life. In each case, such persons would

divide their time between actual teaching (or some other form of cultural productivity) and the administrative control of the educational system. It will be evident to anyone who can bring himself to an unbiased examination of cultural life that the peculiar vitality and energy of soul required for organizing and directing educational institutions will be called forth only in someone actively engaged in teaching or in some sort of cultural creativity.[40]

The pedagogical and didactic teaching of the Waldorf School should receive its impulse from a true spiritual scientific understanding of people. . . .

[W]e must build all pedagogical art on a knowledge of the soul that is closely tied to the personality of the teacher. This personality must be able to freely express itself in pedagogical creativity. That, however, is possible only if the entire administration of the school system is autonomous, if practicing teachers need to deal only with other practicing teachers in administrative questions. An educator not actively teaching would be just as much out of place in the school administration as a person without artistic creativity would be in giving directions to creative artists. The nature of the pedagogical art requires that the faculty divide its time between teaching and administering the school. The spirit formed out of the attitude of all teachers united in an educating community thus comes to full effect in the administration. In this community only what comes from a recognition, an understanding, of the soul will have value.

Such a community is possible only in the Threefold Social Organism, which has a free cultural life alongside a democratically oriented state and an independent economic life. . . . A cultural life that receives its directives from the political bureaucracy or from the forces of economic life cannot take care of a school whose impulse derives solely from the faculty.[41]

You might have been wondering which kind of people would make good teachers in a [Waldorf] school. They are people whose entire lives have been molded by the spiritual knowledge of which I spoke. . . .

Those who believe in the anthroposophical way of life must insist on a free and independent cultural-spiritual life. This represents one of the three branches of the threefold social [organism]. . . . One of the demands that must be made for spiritual life—something that is not at all utopian, that may be begun any day—is that those actively engaged in spiritual life (and this means, above all, those involved in its most important public domain, namely education) should also be entrusted with all administrative matters, and this in a broad and comprehensive way.

The maximum number of lessons to be taught—plus the hours spent on other educational commitments—should allow teachers sufficient time for regular meetings, in both smaller and larger groups, to deal with administrative matters. However, only practicing teachers— not former teachers now holding state positions or retired teachers— should be called on to care for this side of education. For what has to be administered in each particular school—as in all institutions belonging to the spiritual-cultural life—should be only a continuation of what is being taught, of what forms the content of every word spoken and every deed performed in the classroom. Rules and regulations must not be imposed from outside the school. In spiritual life, autonomy, self-administration, is essential.[42]

The cardinal ideas within, and which can be deduced from, these quotations are:

- The Waldorf teaching methods are developed out of a spiritual-scientific knowledge of the human being, including the soul-spiritual aspect of the child. Rightly considered, this knowledge becomes a part of the personality of the teacher, who must be able to work freely and creatively in relation to the students. This can occur only if schools are not directed by the State in matters of content and manner of teaching. Therefore, school administration, including curriculum, goals, and standards, need to be completely removed from State control. (See Chapter 16 for appropriate relation of the state to schooling.)

- The educational system and the rest of cultural life should constitute an independent branch of social life with its own administration and governance system. Education is the primary value-forming aspect of culture, out of which all culture—science, art, and religion—evolves.

- School administration, as expressed here, should be viewed in a broad and comprehensive manner to include the whole educational system at all levels from nursery programs to the highest level of universities and trade schools. When speaking of administration, Steiner does not speak solely about individual schools but rather about the entire educational system. Steiner's indications regarding self-administration gain meaning only when they are viewed in the context of the movement for independent education and a threefold social organism.

- To preclude any possibility of outside interference of the educational system by political and economic forces, only active teachers or other cultural workers should be making administrative decisions. Teachers' workloads should not only allow them the time to participate in administration in a particular school but also the administering of the whole educational system and cultural life.

- Administration should be an extension and reflection of what takes place and arises out of the classroom rather than the life of the classroom being shaped by an administration subordinate to political and economic forces.

- Teachers should be as capable in administrative matters as they are in the classroom. A community of educators will arise out of the dynamics of an administration of the educational system based on the understanding and recognition of the soul. This community of educators will oversee the goals and standards of education.

In keeping with the principle of freedom and individual responsibility, Steiner instituted what he called the republican approach to administration. He described this approach to the new teachers just before the launching of the first Waldorf school as follows:

Two opposite forces have to be harmonized in the course of our work. On the one hand we must know what our ideals are [pedagogical and social], yet we must be flexible enough to adapt ourselves to things that are far removed from our ideals. The difficult task of harmonizing these two forces stands before each of you. And you will only achieve this if you engage all the forces of your personality. Each of you will have to put your whole personality into it right from the start.

The school, therefore, will have its own administration run on a republican basis and will not be administered from above. We must not lean back and rest securely on the orders of a headmaster; we must be a republic of teachers and kindle in ourselves the strength that will enable us to do what we have to do with full responsibility. Each one of you, as an individual, has to be fully responsible.[43]

There are two aspects of the modern concept of *republican* relevant to a Waldorf school. First, all members are considered equals, and second, the ultimate ruling body (the carrying teachers in the case of a Waldorf school) has the power to elect or appoint representatives to take on specific duties on their behalf. Steiner wanted the teachers to be jointly responsible for the decision-making and administrative execution of decisions with the full weight of their personalities. In a modern Waldorf school this translates for the most part into a faculty-run governance system, mandated committees, and appointed administrators headed by a faculty council or college of teachers.

Without going immediately into the actual challenges and problems that often occur in Waldorf schools trying to work out of the republican approach, we can already deduce the following from Steiner's perspective on administration:

1) If teachers are to feel just as much at home in administration as they are in teaching, and have the proper understanding of administration in a broad and com-

prehensive way in harmony with the ideals of social threefolding, then all three areas—pedagogy, social threefolding, including educational freedom, and administration—would need to be given equal emphasis in teacher-training institutes and programs.

2) In order for teachers to have time to deal with administrative matters, sufficient funds in the school budget would be necessary to keep work loads at an appropriate level.

In a later chapter we will review some of the more obvious problems that have occurred in the administrative areas of Waldorf schools.

ꙮ

CHAPTER 6

PRIVATE FUNDING: WHY AND HOW

Independent education, like all education, needs to be financed with an ongoing stream of money. The logical next question is: How is it possible to obtain the amount of money required in such a way that a school can retain its freedom and still be accessible to students of all economic backgrounds? As we have learned, Steiner tried a number of ways to develop multiple private-sector income streams for the first Waldorf school. He had hoped these would eventually develop into a steady river of support, but there never seemed to be enough money.

It was inevitable that the question of government support for independent schools should arise in relation to Waldorf education. In 1917, two years prior to the founding of the first Waldorf school, Holland passed a law that provided for government financial support of private schools. During a discussion period after a lecture in 1922, a teacher asked Rudolf Steiner about starting a Waldorf school in Holland with government subsidies. Steiner rejected the idea because he felt that a state subsidized-school could not remain free of government control.

Questioner: According to Dutch law it is possible to found a free school, if the government is satisfied of the serious and genuine intentions behind such an impulse. If we in Holland were unable to raise the necessary capital for founding a Waldorf school, would it be right for us to accept state subsidies, as long as we were allowed to arrange our curriculum and our lessons according to Waldorf principles?

Rudolf Steiner: There is one part of the question I do not understand, and another which fills me with doubts. What I cannot understand is that in Holland it should not be possible to get enough money together for a really free school. Forgive me if I am naïve, but I do not understand it. For I believe that, if there is enough enthusiasm, it should at least be possible to start such a school. After all, not so very much money is needed to start a school.

The other point which seems dubious to me is that it should be possible to run a [free] school with the aid of State subsidies. For I very much doubt whether the government, if it pays out money for such a school, would not insist on the right to inspect it. Therefore I cannot believe that a free school could be founded with State subsidies which in themselves imply supervision by inspectors of the education authorities.[44]

Steiner did acknowledge that it was appropriate for the State to take over the provision of education from the various religions for a period of time to allow for the development of human freedom. But he also maintained that to persist in this arrangement poses a grave threat to human culture.[45] The democratic principles of equality and majority rule are no longer appropriate in matters of education where individual perspectives and choices should hold sway. Steiner maintained, therefore, that financial support for education should come directly from the economy by way of individuals and organizations, and not be detoured through the state, where it would be subject to majority rule (or worse yet, powerful interest groups).

One might then think: If the state, through its coercive powers, no longer pays the teachers what they need, then it would go badly for the teachers. But the teachers will belong to an economic corporation, similar to other economic corporations. Along with being teachers they will also be members of the third aspect of the threefold social organism (the economic aspect), and will receive salaries from that independent economic system. The threefold social organism will have an independent

economic body, just as it has an independent legal body that will demo-
cratically take care of legal matters. Similarly, it will also have a free
spiritual realm. What today goes into the pockets of teachers indirectly
through taxes will, in the future, come directly from the economic life.
Apart from that, a free spiritual life will foster the appropriate atmo-
sphere for schools and teaching.[46]

He described once how he was chided by a person in the audi-
ence following one of his lectures because of this position. The
person asserted that the poor German people could not afford to
fund education and that the State was the only source of the large
amount of money required. In response, Steiner pointed out that
the State does not generate wealth. Therefore, even the State would
have to rely on the economy of the poor nation as the source of
funds.

I was answered in the discussion at the end of a lecture by a sec-
ondary school teacher, somewhat in this wise: "We Germans shall be a
poor nation in the future, and here is a man who wants to make the
spiritual and intellectual life independent; a poor people cannot pay
for that, there will be no money, therefore we shall have to draw on the
national exchequer and pay for education out of the taxes. What be-
comes of independence then? How can we refuse the right of the State
to inspect, when the State is the source of income?"

I could only reply that it seemed strange to me for the teacher to
believe that what was drawn from the Treasury as taxes grew there
somehow or other, and would not in the future come out of the pocket
of the "poor nation." What strikes me most is the lack of thought every-
where. We need to develop a real practical thinking which sees into the
facts of life. That will give us practical suggestions which can be carried
out.[47]

Although he agreed that all children have a right to an education, Steiner considered the so-called tuition free school—public
or private—a social lie. In reality, some person, or group, must
have amassed the capital to fund schools either privately or through
taxes. In either case, the purse holder controls the education.

Throughout the land today you hear the cry for schooling free of charge. What does this really imply? But the cry throughout the land should be: How can we get a form of socialism in which everyone is enabled to contribute in the right way towards educational affairs? Free schooling is nothing less than a social lie, for behind this is hidden either the fact that surplus value finds its way into the pockets of a small set of people who then found a school and thus gain mastery over others; or sand is strewn in the eyes of the public so that they should not realize that among the coins they take from their purse there must be some that go to the upkeep of schools. In all that we say, in the very shaping of our sentences, we must conscientiously strive after truth.[48]

From a threefold perspective, the right to an education means that a family has the financial means to have its children educated in the school or program of its choice. "The necessary capital must be provided . . . for the education of those who are not yet productive. . . . The education and support of those who are incapable of working is something which concerns all humanity, and through a rights-state detached from the economy, it will be so. . . ."[49] How does one make sure that there are sufficient funds for the education of all children without education being subjected to outside control?

Steiner suggests two approaches. One is through adjusting or augmenting a person's income if he or she has school-age children. This could be introduced to a certain degree through various legal measures connected to wage laws. Another possibility is that the State would require that sufficient money be set aside by the economy for education—perhaps into education funds or foundations—and would also determine who would be eligible to access the funds (establishing student age limits and family income requirements, for example). The point is that the money does not pass through the government, but the State does ensure that sufficient funds are available to those who need them. Although it appears that we are a long way off from such arrangements, there are social movements in harmony with these ideas that could be strengthened, such as privately-funded voucher programs and the universal living wage movement.

Before going further in our exploration of Waldorf education, we will now give a brief overview of government education reform in the United States since the early 1980s. The reason for this apparent digression is to understand how completely contrary these reform efforts are to the ideals of educational freedom and the three-fold social organism, and to highlight the necessity for Waldorf education to reconnect to its original social mission of leading a movement for true educational freedom. Whereas it is time for government and business to be withdrawing from the control of education, it will be shown that for the last twenty or more years big business and the federal and state governments in the United States have pushed for a uniform, centrally-controlled, nationalized educational system. In so doing, these interests often use alluring terms to support their goals and actions such as parental choice, educational freedom, diversity, and local control. However, their way of characterizing and implementing these actions are a distortion of truth. After reviewing this sharp contrast to the social mission of Waldorf education, we will once again return to our central theme of independence, private funding, and accessibility for independent schools.

PART II

U.S. EDUCATION REFORM: 1981–2002

෨෪

CHAPTER 7

A NATION AT RISK

We shall focus our exploration of federal educational reform efforts by reviewing a series of events that have taken place since the early 1980s, including the 1983 report "A Nation at Risk," the four subsequent national education summits, relevant federal legislation, and the influence of the *national* Business Roundtable (BRT).

On August 26, 1981, T.H. Bell, the Secretary of Education under President Ronald Reagan, established the National Commission on Excellence in Education because there was a "widespread perception that something is seriously remiss in our educational system." This commission was directed to find out what was wrong and suggest solutions to the problems. Approximately eighteen months later, the Commission issued the report, "A Nation at Risk: The Imperative for Educational Reform," which sent shock waves throughout the nation. It declared that we were facing a national crisis in education, particularly from an economic perspective.

Our once unchallenged preeminence in commerce, industry, science, and technological innovation is being overtaken by competitors throughout the world. This report is concerned with only one of the many causes and dimensions of the problem, but it is the one that undergirds American prosperity, security, and civility. . . . [T]he educational foundations of our society are presently being eroded by a ris-

ing tide of mediocrity that threatens our very future as a Nation and a people. What was unimaginable a generation ago has begun to oc-cur—others are matching and surpassing our educational attainments.

If an unfriendly foreign power had attempted to impose on America the mediocre educational performance that exists today, we might well have viewed it as an act of war. . . . The risk is not only that the Japanese make automobiles more efficiently than Americans and have government subsidies for development and export. It is not just that the South Koreans recently built the world's most efficient steel mill, or that American machine tools, once the pride of the world, are being displaced by German products. It is also that these developments signify a redistribution of trained capability throughout the globe. Knowl-edge, learning, information, and skilled intelligence are the new raw materials of international commerce and are today spreading through-out the world as vigorously as miracle drugs, synthetic fertilizers, and blue jeans did earlier. If only to keep and improve on the slim competi-tive edge we still retain in world markets, we must dedicate ourselves to the reform of our educational system for the benefit of all.[50]

A 1992 article in *Newsweek* described with hindsight the pro-gressive development of educational concerns from national con-sciousness to seeking national solutions, including national test-ing.

The shot heard round the educational world was fired in 1983, with the publication of "A Nation at Risk." After that widely publi-cized federal report described education as a national crisis, it became more acceptable to think of national solutions. At the same time, Ameri-can school officials, reacting to public concern about global competi-tion, began looking overseas to see how other countries educated their future workers. They found that countries whose students scored high-est on international tests all had a planned curriculum. In some coun-tries, such as France or Germany, the education ministries control the lesson plans through national tests, which determine whether students move up to universities or go out into the work force. The curriculum is geared to the tests. In Japan, the government strictly screens school text-books, giving it a virtual lock on what is taught in the classroom.[51]

It is quite obvious that the wording of the "A Nation at Risk" report was calculated to create an effect in the soul of the reader, a nation-wide fear that would require a nation-wide treatment. Indeed, the report was a complete success in this regard. It sent politicians, educators, and business leaders across the nation into a frenzy of research and reform. Hundreds of reports were issued suggesting ways out of our educational crisis, and hundreds of educational reform programs at all levels were implemented throughout the country. Business-education partnerships increased from 42,200 to 140,800 from 1983 to 1988, according to the February 1989 report by the National Center for Education Statistics.

However, the results of the reform programs, research papers, and partnerships with schools were far from satisfactory. Nearly all assessments showed that there was very little progress in the improvement of educational quality; if anything, we were going backward. There seemed to be no consensus on what it would take to improve education. That is, not until 1989.

જી

FIRST NATIONAL EDUCATION SUMMIT
AND "AMERICA 2000"

In 1989, President George Bush and the fifty state governors met at an educational summit in Virginia. They agreed to establish six national goals for education to give a focus and direction to our national educational consciousness and reform efforts. The six educational goals established by the President and the governors were to be reached by the year 2000. See Illustration 2.

> Illustration 2
> The Original Six National Education Goals Established in 1989
> *1. All children in America will start school ready to learn.*
> *2. The high school graduation rate will increase to at least 90%.*
> *3. American students will leave grades four, eight, and twelve having demonstrated competency in challenging subject matter, including English, mathematics, science, history, and geography; and every school in America will ensure that all students learn to use their minds well, so that they may be prepared for responsible citizenship, further learning, and productive employment in our modern economy.*
> *4. U.S. students will be the first in the world in science and mathematics achievement.*

> 5. Every adult in America will be literate and will possess the knowledge and skills necessary to compete in a global economy and exercise the rights and responsibilities of citizenship.
> 6. Every school in America will be free of drugs and violence and will offer a disciplined environment conducive to learning.[52]

It is worth noting that none of these goals was achieved by the year 2000 as originally intended.

To many people these goals seem rather inoffensive. They do not have any objection to children starting school "ready to learn," or to our high school graduation rate increasing to "at least 90%" or to "every adult in America" being literate and having the skills needed for work. And what person in his right mind would object to all schools being free of violence and drugs? But to get to the reality of the potentially harmful effect of these goals we need to ask: How is it possible to translate these general goals into concrete reality? How can we determine whether we are making progress towards these goals, and what will be our assessment methods? The responses to these questions, regardless of the specific answers, will only lead to greater control of education by the State and the economy.

America 2000

In April 1991, President George Bush and Secretary of Education Lamar Alexander announced "America 2000," a nine-year strategy to achieve the six goals. The strategy was developed supposedly to honor local school control, create partnerships between local government and the private sector, and build on the conviction that improvements in American education should develop community by community.

In keeping with the Education 2000 program, President Bush began pushing the idea of *voluntary* national testing to assess the progress of the students, teachers, and schools in striving toward the national goals in order to establish "better and more accountable schools." On June 27, 1991, Congress, with the backing of the President and the National Association of Governors, established the National Council on Education Standards and Testing to consider the desirability and feasibility of national educational standards:

The Council concluded that standards and tests were essential to reach the educational goals that the President and the nation's governors have set for the year 2000. These include making American children the best in the world in mathematics and science achievement and insuring that they demonstrate competency in five core subjects: English, mathematics, science, history, and geography. . . . Although such standards and tests would be voluntary, the Council recommended incentives for states and local school districts to adopt them, such as tying federal scholarships to test results, or penalties for schools that have high failure rates.[53]

Bush also prodded business leaders to help create a new generation of schools through to establishing a not-for-profit corporation, New American Schools Development Corporation (NASDC), to create model schools that set the standard for achieving the national goals. In addition, Bush also announced a proposal for a federal voucher program offering $1,000 for each school-age child to enable parents to send their children to the schools of their choice. These vouchers were intended to accelerate the acceptance of national goals, standards, and testing in all schools, public and private. The voucher proposal, however, failed to gain legislative approval.

ɘʃ

CHAPTER 9

THE NATIONAL BUSINESS ROUNDTABLE (BRT)

None of the previously mentioned reform efforts and the ones that follow can be clearly understood without knowing about the influence of the *national* Business Roundtable (BRT). The BRT is an association of approximately one hundred fifty chief executive officers (CEOs) of leading U.S. businesses. "The Roundtable is committed to advocating public policies that ensure vigorous economic growth."[54] In general, its methods are to develop task forces on specific issues, direct research, recommend policy, and lobby Congress and the President's administration to implement their wishes.

Following the publication of "A Nation at Risk," the BRT encouraged its member companies to become actively involved in educational reform, particularly through the business-education partnerships previously mentioned. Not satisfied with the overall progress of the reform effort, the BRT's Public Policy Committee met in September 1988 and "discussed the critical importance of business leadership in partnerships with education and the powerful role that can and must be played by the CEOs of the Roundtable. There was general agreement on the need to move ahead with personal, direct action, using corporate resources to help stimulate educational reform"[55]

The BRT's initial strategy is described in a report published in April 1988, *The Role of Business in Education Reform: Blueprint for Action.* A two-level strategy was recommended:

"Involve the Business Roundtable as a *national organization* in education public policy mainly on the federal level.

"Promote Roundtable *member company* activity in school/business programs and *member company* involvement in public policy issues mainly on the state and local levels."[56] The Business Roundtable responded to the premise of "A Nation at Risk" report that education is to be viewed primarily in economic terms:

The rationale is clear. How well we educate all of our children will determine our competitiveness globally, our economic health domestically and our communities' character and vitality. While American education has made undeniable progress in recent years, the pace of this progress is not keeping up with the pace of change in business, technology, and commerce.[57]

The Blueprint for Action recommended that the BRT should "make a sustained commitment to education through a CEO-led effort" and also "should influence education at the federal level, including the subject of national curriculum standards."[58]

Furthermore, "Roundtable companies should endorse public policy issues at the state and local levels that encourage focus on issues such as curriculum standards, teacher competency, and teacher compensation."[59] And the BRT mounted an "effort to assure that at least one of its members be committed to working with the governor of each state and the District of Columbia over the next ten years to help improve that state's and the District's education system."[60]

But it was not until the national educational goals were established that the BRT saw a way to focus its efforts on education in a directed and systematic manner: "With the establishment of national education goals, business has a unique opportunity to work with state and local education officials on establishing state and local goals, objectives and standards. Business can collaborate with educators on building state-wide strategies and policies for the implementation of these goals. In addition, business can be a catalyst for this effort, as well as a central player on the panels, commissions and committees that will make recommendations and oversee a state's activities to ensure that the goals and objectives are reached."[61]

Over the years the Business Roundtable has been blunt about the connection its strategy has to the national educational goals:

We have been learning more about the issues, generating additional and deeper commitment on many fronts and working with the President, the governors, and other interested parties in the formulation of the announced educational goals. We support the goals. Their achievement is vital to the nation's well-being. Now it is time to begin implementation—state by state—recognizing that no single improvement will bring about the systematic change that is needed. The effort requires a comprehensive approach that utilizes the knowledge and resources of broadly based partnerships in each state. The next step is to agree on action plans for a public policy agenda that defines the characteristics of a successful school system. This paper identifies those essential system components, which we see as the requirements for provoking the degree of change necessary for achieving the national goals through successful schools. Individual Roundtable CEOs and the governors have teamed up to institute these components in state policy. The action plan for each state will be measured against how the plan contributes to or detracts from these essential components. The nine components should be considered as a comprehensive and integrated whole. While their implementation should be strategically phased in, if any one is left unattended, the chances of overall success will be sharply reduced.[62]

The nine essential components referred to are: standards, assessment, accountability, professional development, school autonomy, technology, learning readiness, parent involvement, and safety and discipline. It is important to realize that all of the components are viewed as part of an all-encompassing "comprehensive and integrated" package. Instead of reviewing the nine components, we will focus on a few underlying thoughts.

- *The new system is performance- or outcomes-based, in contrast to our present reliance on inputs.*

Hitherto, public education was based on conforming to rules and regulations in order to receive government money. The new BRT-endorsed approach shifts the emphasis from inputs, or mere adherence to rules or procedures, to results, outcomes, or performance. "Too often, our school staffs are asked, 'Did you do what you were told?' The right question is: 'What did students learn?' Trying hard is not enough. What students actually know and can do—student performance—is what counts. Our society must define, in measurable terms, the required results for students and work relentlessly work toward them."[63]

Another important reason given by the BRT for shifting to outcomes-based education is that it can streamline the enactment of reform measures by eliminating the bureaucratic wrangling that occurs at various levels. By shifting to outcomes or performance-based national education policy, the implementation of administrative actions can be narrowed down to a centralized goals-implemented body whose responsibility would include formulating national standards and tests: The magazine *Newsweek* summarized the situation this way: "It's unlikely that any federal agency will try to force changes in the classroom. Districts will probably still be autonomous, but there will be tremendous outside pressure to get with the program. A national quasi-governmental agency, such as the standards council, could coordinate teacher accreditation, development of standards, and testing."[64]

- *Assessment strategies must be as strong and rich as the outcomes.*

If the outcomes must be defined in measurable terms, and if these outcomes are in reality in keeping with national goals, assessment methods will have to be produced to assure that the students' performances are really meeting the standards. National goals inevitably require national assessment, that is, national tests and specific national standards. Tests inevitably influence what is taught.

- *Schools should receive awards for success, assistance for improvments, and penalties for failure.*

If an educational system is to be based on outcomes, then there must be some way of ensuring that all the participants do everything possible to achieve the pre-determined results. Outcomes-based education goes hand in hand with behavioristic reinforcement techniques: "A system built on high standards requires consequences for schools and school employees based on demonstrated performance. There must be incentives to encourage continual improvement, rewards for success, and penalties for failure."[65]

- *School-based staff have a major role in making instructional decisions.*

Because they carry the responsibility for making sure that children meet outcome standards in keeping with national goals, teachers and other staff will be given a greater say in instruction technique and local management to achieve the outcomes dictated to them by the state. Under school-based management, states and central school districts should retain the authority to set overall goals, standards, and expectations for student performance, but decisions on methods to accomplish these ends should be left to the schools and teachers.

In other words, the teachers on a local level shall give up all jurisdiction over the direction and goals of education and in exchange will receive a comparatively deregulated space in which to meet the required outcomes. This has been referred to as *procedural freedom.*

- *Technology is used to raise student and teacher productivity and to expand the learning process.*

A performance-driven, outcomes-based educational system that embraces one set of uniform goals for every student, and all educational institutions will require the heavy and pervasive use of technology at all levels of schools in order to meet the desired results: "Technology is a powerful tool for teaching, learning and school management. It must be a critical part of the comprehensive change needed to achieve high standards."[66]

In the 1999 report, "No Turning Back," Edward B. Rust, Jr., chairman of State Farm Insurance and chairman of the BRT Education Task Force, outlined the achievements and determination of the BRT to shape American education to its vision. The following words show without a shadow of doubt that federal and state education policy is primarily determined by corporate America by using coercive economic power through threats and philanthropic incentives.

Although the job is far from finished, there is much to show for our work with governors, legislators, educators, and other business leaders.

We focused on changing public policy in the states, where the U.S. Constitution assigns primary responsibility for education leadership.[67] We insisted that policymakers and educators begin measuring progress based on bottom line gains in student achievement (results). . . .

We spurred Comprehensive Policy Changes through a nine-point reform agenda, with high standards as the centerpiece. We emphasized comprehensive changes to all the interrelated parts of the K-12 educational system. We are not satisfied with piecemeal reforms. . . .

The business community focused its initial attention on the core elements of standards, assessment and accountability—the basic foundation for improvement. . . .

On the national level, the BRT took the lead in establishing the Business Coalition for Educational Reform, now a thirteen-member group that serves as a unified voice for the corporate community, and in developing a Common Agenda for reform endorsed by the business community. . . . Today, Roundtable companies are at the forefront of a national effort by businesses to stimulate academic progress by aligning their hiring, philanthropic and site location practices with our education reform agenda . . . .

It has been said that large organizations such as schools "don't change because they see the light; they change because they feel the heat."

Business Roundtable CEOs have successfully applied the heat on state policymakers, while state coalitions are helping the public and educators see the light about the need for change. We need to keep it up until all students have the knowledge and skills to participate fully in the civic, social and economic world in which they live.

The history of past reform attempts is very clear on this point. If we believe that school reform is vital to the success of America, we cannot—and will not—leave the job to others. There can be no turning back.[68]

There cannot be a clearer description of the role that big business has played in relation to education reform in the U.S. during the last part of the twentieth century.

ॐ

CHAPTER 10

GOALS 2000: EDUCATE AMERICA Act

Regardless of the many apparent differences the Republican and Democratic parties may have in their political perspectives and platforms, one thing they are in complete accord with is the need for education reform centered around national goals, standards, and testing. When William Clinton defeated George Bush, Sr., and replaced him as President of the United States, he intensified the federal government's efforts in this direction with the passage of the "Goals 2000: Educate America Act," which codified eight national education goals.[69] Two more goals were added to the six that were endorsed by the nation's governors at the 1989 Educational Summit. The two additions set goals for teacher development and parental involvement in their children's education.[70] "Goals 2000" provided for a massive array of measures to assist and encourage the states to "voluntarily" attain the eight goals by the year 2000. The Act reauthorized all federal funding for education in conjunction with the national educational goals. See Illustration 3 for purposes of the Act.

Illustration 3

Purpose of the "Goals 2000: Educate America Act"

The purpose of this Act is to provide a framework for meeting the National Educational Goals established by Title 1 of this Act by —
 1. promoting coherent, nationwide, systemic education reform;

---

2. *improving the quality of learning and teaching in the class-room and in the workplace;*

3. *defining appropriate and coherent Federal, State and local roles and responsibilities for education reform and lifelong learning;*

4. *establishing valid and reliable mechanisms for—*

   (a) building a broad national consensus on American education reform;

   (b) assisting in the development and certification of high-quality, internationally competitive content and student performance standards;

   (c) assisting in the development and certification of opportunity-to-learn standards; and

   (d) assisting in the development and certification of high-quality assessment measures that reflect the international competitive content and student performance standard;.

5. *supporting new initiatives at the Federal, State, local and school levels to provide equal educational opportunity for all students to meet high academic and occupational skill standards and to succeed in the world of employment and civic participation;*

6. *providing a framework for the reauthorization of all Federal education programs by:*

   (a) creating a vision of excellence and equity that will guide all Federal education and related programs;

   (b) providing for the establishment of high-quality, internationally competitive content and student performance standards and strategies that all students will be expected to achieve;

   (c) providing for the establishment of high-quality, internationally competitive opportunity-to-learn standards that all state and local educational agencies and schools should achieve;

   (d) encouraging and enabling all state and local educational agencies to develop comprehensive improvement plans that

will provide a coherent framework for the implementation of reauthorized federal education and related programs in an integrated fashion that effectively educate all children to prepare them to participate fully as workers, parents, and citizens;

(e) providing resources to help individual schools, including those serving students with high needs, develop and implement comprehensive improvement plans; and

(f) promoting the use of technology to enable all students to achieve the National Education Goals.

7. stimulating the development and adoption of a voluntary national system of skills standards and certification to serve as a cornerstone of the national strategy to enhance workforce skills; and

8. assisting every elementary and secondary school that receives funds under this Act to actively involve parents and families in supporting the academic work of their children at home and in providing parents with the skills to advocate for their children at school.[71]

It is interesting to note that the action verbs describing the purposes of the Act focus on *promoting, supporting, encouraging, enabling, assisting, stimulating,* which have the character of outside assistance without control. Also, the authors of the Act abundantly use the term *voluntary* to avoid any legal challenges. That is because, according to the U.S. Constitution, the federal government has no legal power over education.

In order for the states to continue accessing hundreds of millions of dollars each year, which they have become dependent on through the federal government programs, they have no choice but to accede to the directives of the federal government. The use of the word *voluntary* is a lie. In essence, with the passage of the "Goals 2000: Educate America Act," the principle of enumerated powers and the separation of powers provided for in the U. S. Constitution were completely abandoned.[72] The Federal government is poised to gain complete control over all K–12 public education. Read Illustration 4, for example, to see how often the term *voluntary* (emphasis added) is used under Title II, Part B, Sec. 211, on the purpose of the National Education Standards and Improvement Council.

Illustration 4

The Purpose of the National Education and
Improvement Council under the
Goals 2000: Educate America Act

The purpose of the Council is to provide for a mechanism to (emphasis added):

1. *certify and periodically review **voluntary** national content standards and **voluntary** national student performance standards that define what all students should know and be able to do;*

2. *certify state content standards and state student performance standards submitted by states on a **voluntary** basis, if such standards are comparable or higher in rigor and quality to the **voluntary** national content standards and **voluntary** national student performance standards certified by the National Education Standards and Improvement Council;*

3. *certify and periodically review **voluntary** national opportunity-to-learn standards that describe the conditions of teaching and learning necessary for all students to have a fair opportunity to achieve the knowledge and skills described in the **voluntary** national content standards and the **voluntary** national student performance standards certified by*

---

the National Education Standards and Improvement Council;

*4. certify opportunity-to-learn standards submitted by states on a **voluntary** basis, if such standards are comparable or higher in rigor to the **voluntary** national opportunity-to-learn standards certified by the National Education Standards and Improvement Council; and*

*5. certify state assessments submitted by states or groups of states on a **voluntary** basis, if such assessments :*

(a) are aligned with and support state content standards certified by such Council; and

(b) are valid, reliable and consistent with relevant, nationally recognized, professional and technical standards for assessment when used for their intended purposes.[73]

✥

CHAPTER 11

1996 EDUCATION SUMMIT: CEOS BECOME VISIBLE

A second national education summit took place on March 26 and 27, 1996, at the IBM conference center in Palisades, NY. The summit organizers were Tommy G. Thompson, Governor of Wisconsin, and Louis V. Gerstner, chairman and chief executive officer of IBM and a member of the BRT. At that time Thompson was known for his promotion of tuition vouchers and charter schools along with performance-based reforms in his home state, and Gerstner was active in promoting technology as an essential component of reform.

At the second summit the governors were encouraged to invite a leading CEO from their state to also participate in this summit. This was the first public show of the united political and economic forces that aim to shape all education in the United States.

The Governors and CEOs made a series of commitments as part of the policy statement issued at the conclusion of the conference. Specifically, the governors at the conference committed to "the development and establishment of internationally competitive academic standards, assessments to measure academic achievement, and accountability systems in our states, according to each state's governing structure, within the next two years."

The business leaders committed to "actively support the work of the governors to improve student performance and to develop coalitions of other business leaders in our states to expand this support....We are committed to considering the quality of a state's academic standards and student achievement levels as a high-priority factor in determining business-location decisions."

Jointly, the governors and the business leaders committed to establish a non-governmental measurement and reporting system on how each state is progressing with educational reform measures. This would include publishing and distributing an annual report. The reports would be "released at a high-profile televised media announcement in each state."[74]

They also pledged to create an independent, non-governmental entity to facilitate their work together. Shortly after the summit, Achieve, Inc., was established to serve as a resource center to states on standards, assessments, accountability and technology; to help states benchmark their academic standards and achievement; and to advocate for the improvement of efforts to raise standards and student performance. Louis Gertsner and Tommy Thompson became the co-chairs.

CHAPTER 12

1999 EDUCATION SUMMIT:
PARENTS AND TEACHERS ARRIVE

The third educational summit took place September 30 and October 1, 1999, again at IBM headquarters in Palisades, NY. The event was sponsored by Achieve, Inc., headed by Gerstner and Thompson and co-sponsored by the Business Roundtable, Council of the Great City Schools, Learning Alliance, National Alliance of Business, National Education Goals Panel, and National Governors' Association.

The third education summit marked the first time that educators and parents were part of the dialogue. In addition to one business leader from each state being invited, one educator from each state was also invited. The parents were represented by the National PTA president. Please note that they were included only after all the major goals and benchmarks for education had been determined in the previous educational summits. They are, however, the ones who will have to achieve what the State and big business have thought out. Sandra Feldman, president of the American Federation of Teachers, starkly described the subservient delivery role of teachers in this massive reform effort: "Teachers and principals are not the bad guys. These [educators] are the people who are going to help us deliver on this."[75]

The summit agenda included five areas thast needed to be addressed in order to accelerate the pace of education reform: standards and accountability, better teaching, helping students learn, more choices, and maintaining public support.[76] In a final Action Statement, the governors, business leaders and educators at the 1999 National Education Summit agreed on a set of specific commitments aimed at raising academic standards and performance in every American classroom. See Illustration 5.

Illustration 5

Commitments made by Governors, Business Leaders, and Educators in the 1999 National Education Summit Action Statement

They pledged to improve educator quality by:
- *establishing alternative pathways into the teaching profession to attract the most talented candidates*
- *raising standards for certification to ensure all teachers are prepared to teach to higher academic standards, regardless of their path into the profession*
- *targeting professional development resources on programs designed to help teachers teach to higher academic standards*
- *equipping school teachers with skills to improve instruction and manage organizational change*
- *creating competitive salary structures that attract and retain the best-qualified teachers, rewarding them for skills and performance*

They pledged to help all students achieve high standards by
- *ensuring every school has a rigorous curriculum aligned with state standards and tests*
- *providing low-achieving students with extra help and additional learning time*
- *giving parents more schooling options by expanding public school choices and charter schools*
- *giving schools substantial flexibility and control over personnel and resources while holding them accountable for results*

> *They pledged to strengthen accountability by*
> - *benchmarking states' standards, assessments and achievements*
> - *recognizing and rewarding highly successful schools*
> - *intervening in chronically failing schools*
> - *providing incentives for students to achieve standards by aligning college admissions standards with high school standards and expanding the number of companies using academic records in their hiring decisions.*[77]

There were some illuminating comments made during the conference. Tommy Thompson, Governor of Wisconsin, in a moment of truthfulness, pointed out that the states had no choice regarding whether they wanted to go along with the reforms or not. "It's not going to be easy, because the consequences for those students that don't measure up are severe. But the consequences for the state that doesn't hang in there are even more severe."[78] There are three obvious consequences if a state does not toe the line: it would be virtually cut off from federal funding; it would receive threats by major corporations not to locate new businesses in their state and to move their existing businesses elsewhere; and it would be excoriated in the press. Also, it is clear in the conference report that increased flexibility to schools and giving parents more schooling options through expanded school choices, including charter schools, are linked to increased accountability through curriculum standards and assessments. In other words, the so-called expansion of diversity in educational delivery systems, such as charter schools, are tied to the standards and testing.

Bob Chase, president of the National Education Association, the largest teachers' union in the country, clearly articulated that the educational reform drive is an integrated, systemic program and that parents, teachers, or schools can not pick and choose what they like and do not like from the reform measures; for instance, increased choices or flexibility with rules, without greater accountability, it is simply not an option. "People understand that it's really a package, that you cannot say, 'This will make it happen' or 'That will make it happen.' It's all these things that will make it happen, and the absence of those things will hamper reaching the goal."[79]

At the close of the conference, each state agreed to develop a detailed response to the Summit Action Statement with specific targets and timelines for action, which would be posted on the Achieve, Inc. website: www.achieve.com.

It is interesting to note that the opening paragraph of the summit's 1999 Action Statement refers to the "A Nation at Risk" report, issued 16 years previously with its warning of a "rising tide of mediocrity that threatens our very future as a nation and as a people." The authors acknowledged the obvious "military and economic supremacy" of the United States in 1999 and, consequently, they had to admit that the reasons used to justify the warning call in the "A Nation at Risk" report—the apparent waning of American economic and political supremacy—could no longer be used. However, the report continues:

"We refuse to be lulled into thinking that our recent military and economic supremacy diminishes the need for reform." And the report justifies continuing the reform efforts because the American public wants these efforts to continue. "In fact, the American public demonstrates, in its response to every poll, that it clearly understands that our continued economic vitality, social stability, and quality of life depend on our ability to dramatically improve our schools."[80]

The great assumption is that the federal reform program, crafted and promoted by big business, is the one and only way to improve schools. Organizations like the BRT and the corporations run by its member CEOs launched public relations efforts between 1989 and 1999 to convince the public that a results-oriented national curriculum and testing was the only solution to the education woes that America was apparently experiencing. They were also quick to counter any observed opposition to their agenda with self-serving studies and opinion polls.[81]

CHAPTER 13

2001 EDUCATION SUMMIT: NATIONAL STANDARDS AS THE NORTH STAR

The fourth national education summit again took place at the IBM headquarters in Palisades, NY. Hosted by Achieve, Inc., and its co-chairs, Louis V. Gerstner, Jr., and Governor John Engler of Michigan. (Tommy Thompson, the former co-chair, was no longer Governor of Wisconsin.) For the second time representatives from the political, business, and educational institutions attended.

Following the 1996 summit, academic standards and testing systems were introduced in nearly every state in compliance with the national goals. At the 1999 summit, the capacities of schools and school systems to deliver high standards had been examined with education leaders present for the first time. The 2001 summit focused on what still needed to be done, in particular, about two key challenges that the states, school districts, and schools were facing: "building the capacities of teachers and schools to meet higher standards and expanding testing and accountability systems to provide better data and stronger incentives for high student achievement."[82] The report of the summit on the Achieve, Inc., website lays out the interlocking components of the reform strategy.

"What will it take for states to ensure that every school is high achieving—to ensure that all children receive nothing less than the best education we can provide for them?" That was the challenge the governors, business leaders and educators attending the 2001 National Education Summit put to themselves.

The starting point remains tying challenging academic standards to real accountability for results. Summit participants agreed. Curriculum must be aligned with those standards, and teachers must have the tools and training to teach to them. While the quality of tests is important, the data they provide schools and the public is also vital. Tests must shape instruction by using the standards as targets. Simply put, the standards are the North Star of our efforts to improve schools.[83]

At the end of the 2001 summit, the participants unanimously adopted a National Education Summit Statement of Principles that provided a guide for moving forward. Some of the important themes in the Statement of Principles were:

- All school curriculum and testing, and the training of teachers are to be based on the new rigorous national standards.
- Admissions to colleges, scholarships, and job placement should be aligned with state test results.
- A teacher's position and salary should be competitive and tied to skills and performance.
- If need be, schools should begin preparing children in pre-kindergarten, or offering after school tutoring so that each child's test results meet the state standards. Testing will cover all subjects and all skills that the State deems worth knowing and being able to do.

ॐ

The 2002 "No Child Left Behind Act" (NCLB)

On January 8, 2002, President George W. Bush signed into law his much-touted "No Child Left Behind Act," which he called the cornerstone of his administration. It incorporated and sought to implement through federal funding the main goals and strategies developed in the previous national education summits.

Big business lobbied heavily for its passage through the Business Coalition for Excellence in Education, which consisted of seventy national business organizations and U.S. corporations, to support what it considered the most important principles of reform. According to the Business Roundtable's website, "the Coalition succeeded in having a tremendous impact on the legislation with most of its key recommendations incorporated into the new law."[84] In effect, big business is the author of the "No Child Left Behind Act."

The main thrust of the Act was to provide unprecedented choices for parents and schools and flexibility for states and local educational agencies (LEAs) in using federal education funds in exchange for unprecedented accountability for states, school districts, and schools. The NCLB authorized on average over $19 billion in total annual funding through forty-five federal programs to the states for implementation of federally mandated education reforms. The NCLB is a reauthorization of the Elementary and Secondary Education (ESA) Act of 1965. Under the NCLB, federal funding is tied to "Adequate Yearly Progress (AYP) of students on federally mandated assessments."[85] The ESA initially covered supplemental aid for poor and disadvantaged children in kindergarten through grade twelve, but, as can be seen, now applies to all public school children in elementary and secondary schools. Some of the main features of the NCLB Act are:

- Requiring states to begin implementing statewide accountability systems by enforcing challenging standards in reading and mathematics and by the annual testing of all students in grades 3–8. Requiring testing in other subjects over the next decade.
- Requiring more stringent state evaluation of teachers that focuses on practices to recruit and train high-quality teachers.
- Requiring accountability of schools for student test scores rated against state standards.
- Requiring schools to regularly report student performance data.
- Rewarding schools that show good progress and penalizing schools that do not make adequate yearly progress (AYP).

True to its doggedly persistent character, the Business Roundtable has posted a "Toolkit for Business" on its web page in which it lays out a strategy for continued business pressure in five key areas of the NCLB Act. They are:

1) Academic Standards
2) Public Disclosure of Achievement Data
3) Accountability
4) Alignment of Educational Improvements
5) Teacher Quality[86]

⚒

CHAPTER 15

CONCLUDING THOUGHTS ON U.S EDUCATION REFORM

More and more, we see that competition in the international marketplace is in reality a "battle of the classrooms."[87]

– Norman R. Augustine, CEO,
Lockheed Martin Corporation,
and Chairman, BRT Education
Task Force

The education reform efforts in the United States have developed out of national concerns and have been legally implemented through federally funded programs. The ideology underlying the reforms is rooted in major U.S.-based multinational corporations. This ideology is an extension or expression of the global market economy based on self-interested behavior, the profit motive, economic competition, and the necessity for rapid economic growth.

As we have seen thus far, the development of the reform efforts has proceeded from a systematic and all-inclusive approach that promotes, implements, and monitors an integrated package of reform measures. The political and business proponents of the reforms take the view that if any of the key components are not developed or are disregarded, it would hamper, if not spell doom for, the whole effort. It is all or nothing.

The essential strategy has been to:

1. Create eight national educational goals that set the direction and time frame for educational reform.

2. Use a performance-based approach to analyzing student progress and teacher effectiveness in reaching targeted goals.

3. Create and implement national tests to monitor and determine whether students, teachers, and schools are meeting the national curriculum standards.

4. Create and implement national teaching standards that are linked to the national curriculum standards.

5. Gear college teacher training programs to support the national goals, standards, and testing.

6. Place teachers' salaries on a commission-type, pay-for-performance salary system.

7. Use massive federal funding to "encourage" the states and school districts to "voluntarily" take up reform efforts in order to avoid legal challenges.

8. Use the media to report on national student test scores to intimidate schools, teachers, and students to try harder to improve test scores.

9. Allow more flexibility and minimize government regulations at the school level in exchange for more accountability.

10. Provide more school choices through charter schools, which will be tied to the national standards and assessments.

11. Use corporate-controlled media and think-tank organizations to relentlessly instill the idea in the public's mind that a good education is equivalent to attaining the national standards and achieving high national test scores, and that the lack of parental support for the reform programs is equivalent to educational neglect and an infringement of a child's right to an education.

In 1916, Rudolf Steiner made the following prediction in a lecture in Berlin, Germany:

We can say that the present age is quite well off in comparison to what is yet to come. . . . After the year 2000 will have passed, it will not be long before thinking—not directly, but in a certain sense—will be forbidden. A law will be enacted in America with the purpose of suppressing all individual thinking. . . . A beginning of this is to be seen in the purely materialistic medicine today, where the soul is not permitted to play a role, where only on the basis of external experiments is the human being to be treated like a machine.[88]

If we consider the "A Nation at Risk" report, the four national education summits, the education agenda of the BRT, the "America 2000" program, and the "Goals 2000: Educate America Act" as all preparation for George W. Bush's "No Child Left Behind Act" that was passed in 2002, we can undoubtedly say that the NCLB Act is the very type of law that Steiner predicted would be enacted shortly after the year 2000, a law that has the effect of suppressing all individual thinking. It is significant to note that decades of concerted efforts *by both liberals and conservatives* at the state and federal levels of government were instrumental in bringing about such a law.

The major threats cited in the 1983 "A Nation at Risk" report from the economies of Japan, Germany, and Korea turned out to have no basis. Their economies declined in the ensuing years, while the U.S. economy surged ahead even though we were reportedly losing the "battle of the classrooms," and our government never came close to achieving any of its goals in the set time frame. It is indeed odd that big business is essentially directing education, the most significant value-shaping aspect of our whole cultural life in the U.S. When it comes down to stock prices and shareholder returns, these multinational corporations have no allegiance to our nation or any nation. Their primary goal is to maximize profits and shareholder values. On one level, that is what the whole push for education reform is all about: keeping the existing market economy expanding as rapidly as possible and making money for big business.

Before turning our attention back to the social task of Waldorf education, it is important to recognize that the practical implementation of the national education reform strategy is only in the beginning stages. Testing requirements, for instance, will be phased in over the next decade, and the state education departments are at various stages of progress in their implementation. This explains why presently some states such as Arizona appear to have less stringent testing requirements than New York State, which is more rapidly implementing standardized tests in keeping with the national goals and standards. But as the implementation deadlines take effect, these differences will be reduced to nil.

Now that we have gained an understanding of the thrust of recent U.S. government education reform, we can see how these efforts embody all that the threefold social organism and the Waldorf school movement was intended to counter: the increasing control of education by the state and business. More than ever, an imagination of how education should be developed in keeping with the principles of freedom and equality needs to be put before the public. And there are signs here in the United States that many parents, teachers, and students in all walks of life, in all types of schools, are longing for just such an imagination with which to unite and strive. There is simply no viable view of education being forcefully and systematically presented as an alternative to what big business is promoting though the state and federal governments. It is up to the Waldorf school movement to help develop this new vision and make it known to the public. For the sake of future generations, Waldorf education must take up the causes of independence and accessibility on behalf of all children. And, as will be explained, it is urgent that major steps in this direction begin here and now in the United States of America.

PART III

THE FUTURE OF WALDORF EDUCATION IN THE USA

⚜

CHAPTER 16

BROAD-BASED FUNDING FOR INDEPENDENT SCHOOLS[89]

Independent Waldorf schools in the United States have reached a decisive point in their evolution regarding financing. If the Waldorf school movement here does not develop broad-based private-sector funding, the schools are faced with the following three options:

1. Becoming absorbed into the government-run public educational system by converting to Waldorf-inspired public schools, and as a consequence, becoming subject to national educational goals, standards, and testing.
2. Becoming financially dependent on government funding through voucher or other programs, and as a consequence eventually becoming subject to the same educational goals, standards, and assessments as public schools.
3. Remaining mainly privately funded, but serving primarily the rich and the privileged.

Some independent schools may become creative enough to develop their own local resources and arrangements of funding to the degree that it gives them financial autonomy and a diverse student population, and we applaud such efforts, but we also need to develop broad-based funding that can help expand the Waldorf school movement and independent educational system in general.

Any effort to work toward appropriate broad-based funding for Waldorf education in harmony with threefold ideals needs to take into consideration the following ideas that have been presented thus far. They constitute the basis for a truly independent educational system:

1. Schools need to be self-administered, and their overall administration should arise from individuals working in the field of education, not from the political state.
2. The financial support of teachers and schools should flow directly from the economy through individuals and organizations to the schools and not pass through the government via taxation.
3. Teachers and schools need to be free of political and economic control regarding the goals and content of education.
4. Educational goals, standards, and assessments can arise only from persons active in teaching and administering schools.
5. Parents should be free to choose the schooling approach they think is most suitable for their children.
6. A child's right to an education and the freedom of choice for parents are meaningless unless the parents have sufficient financial resources to pay for their children's schooling.
7. The legitimate functions of the political state regarding the right of a child to an education should be limited to:
   a. Ensuring that children are educated in physically safe conditions and are protected against physical and mental abuse.
   b. Upholding appropriate anti-discrimination laws.
   c. Ensuring that parents are fully informed about school policies, curriculum, student assessment procedures, and teaching methods, and providing parents legal protection against fraudulent claims by schools.

d. Enforcing various contractual arrangements, agreements, and policies related to schooling.

e. Ensuring that sufficient financial resources are transferred from the economy through individuals and organizations to teachers and schools on an annual basis so that *all* children can receive an adequate education.

f. Determining who is eligible to receive money set aside for education, for example, by establishing age criteria and residency requirements.

Independent schools in the United States are for the most part already funded directly or indirectly from economic life through tuition, fees, and gifts. The great problem is that typically there is just not enough support from these sources for them to be accessible to families from all income levels and for teachers and staff to receive an adequate income.

It needs to be acknowledged that even when money is contributed from economic life to education, stipulations or restrictions may be attached to the transfer. This may be the case with corporate giving, individual contributions, or foundation grants. This is not an inherent necessity, however, as in the case of government funding. Public funding derived from taxes *requires* public oversight whereas private sector funding *may or may not* have strings attached. In the latter instance, the restrictions are more a matter of social consciousness, while in the former it is a matter of the nature and functioning of a modern state.[90]

A notable exception to this perspective in economic life is contributions from publicly-traded stock companies. They are similar to government agencies in that one can expect certain stipulations or requirements attached to their support of education. This is because the management of such corporations is essentially legally required to base all major decisions on what will maximize shareholder values. Consequently, major corporate giving tends toward self-serving marketing and advertising rather than being altruistic contributions dedicated to the general needs of children and society.

No matter what approach one takes in developing broad-based private funding for independent schools, all efforts must be accompanied, if not preceded, by an ongoing, organized effort to educate the public about the importance and necessity of freedom in education as espoused here. This is of paramount importance. Without such efforts, even the most carefully constructed funding mechanism with guards against unwanted and unwarranted external control of education will of necessity degenerate into tools for coercion. No mechanism or technique will work for long; no law, no regulation, not even a constitutional amendment is secure against political and economic forces unless there is a complementary striving to educate the mind and influence the sentiment of the public, albeit in a free way, regarding the ideal of educational freedom. Furthermore, in order for this enlightenment process to develop the necessary social force, and for people to develop the necessary discernment, it must include the recognition of the spiritual basis of the human being and human evolution.

Assuming that a significant effort is made to educate the public regarding the importance of educational freedom, the great question and challenge is how one can work in a practical way to take at least beginning steps toward developing significantly greater broad-based funding for independent schools.

One such effort to make more funds available and alleviate some of the financial stress of parents who want to exercise their school choice options is the *privately-funded* voucher movement. The first such program was started in the United States in 1991 by the Golden Rule Insurance Company in Indianapolis, Indiana. There are now dozens of such programs in the U.S. Simply stated, they are not-for-profit, charitable organizations set up to fundraise for and award scholarship money to students from low-income families who want to send their children to a private school of their choice. They have proven to be both effective and efficient mechanisms, but suffer from two problems. One is that the demand for such scholarships greatly exceeds the ability of the foundations to raise funds. This illustrates in very real terms the desire of many parents to send their children to private schools. The other problem is that the movement has become heavily influenced by special interests and parties who want to use the private programs as case studies and public relations tools to support their political agenda of creating *government funded* voucher programs. *This is an example of what we have suggested will happen when an effort to expand private sector funding is not linked to an equivalent effort to promote the idea of educational freedom.* What is otherwise a very positive step becomes undermined and diverted to the powers opposing true educational freedom. Nonetheless, there are private voucher foundations that are not politically motivated. Such funding organizations could still be important components in a long-term strategy to develop broad-based funding for independent schools if they are linked to both the principles of teacher and school autonomy and freedom of choice for parents.

An interesting development has arisen out of the private voucher movement in the state of Arizona. Like all private voucher programs, the Arizona School Choice Trust was faced with many more families requesting financial assistance than it could help. In order to broaden the support of private voucher programs, individuals connected with the Trust helped initiate legislation in the State of Arizona that allowed citizens to take part of their financial support of education and give it to a charitable organization of their choice that offers private school tuition support. According to Arizona legislation passed in 1998, individuals can contribute up to $500 and married couples who file a joint return can contribute up to $625 to a recognized school tuition organization and have their state tax obligation be reduced by the same amount, dollar for dollar, through a tax credit. In effect, this can be viewed as a step toward acknowledging every adult's obligation to support the education of children, while introducing an element of free choice as to where they can apply the funds and in what form: government taxes or personal contributions. Five hundred or six hundred fifty dollars might seem to be rather insignificant amounts, but some schools have derived hundreds of thousands of dollars through the tax credit program on behalf of eligible families receiving scholarships in a single school year. So far, the tax credit system in Arizona places no additional restrictions on private schools, and the obligations placed on the school tuition organizations are limited to such requirements as using at least ninety percent of the tax credit funds for scholarships. Again, this could change for the worse if there is not a concerted effort to educate the public about the role and importance of independent education in modern life.

Other states have also introduced educational tax credits, but there is a significant variation in their forms. Some, for instance, apply only to contributions made by corporations rather than individuals. Each one would have to be analyzed individually as to its worthiness. Whether any particular tax credit proposal is, as some people describe, a government voucher program in sheep's clothing or a lionhearted effort to take a step toward placing education on an appropriate financial basis will depend on the thoughts and ideals that underlie its formation, implementation, and defense. Undoubtedly, it will be necessary to develop and define a term other than *tax credit* in order to distinguish approaches that are striving for true educational freedom and threefold ideals from those that are political traps. A new term should be defined to give such contributions for the education of children a validity in their own right so that they are not viewed as a credit on, or variation of, the existing tax system. Rather, these contributions should be viewed as a legitimate way for persons or organizations to fulfill their obligation to support the education of children: in other words, an entirely new and valid option to support the right of a child to an education. This would be in harmony with Steiner's idea that money should flow from individuals and organizations in economic life directly to schools rather than through the government via taxes. For discussion purposes here, let us use the acronym "VASE "standing for "valid alternative support of education" for this new educational funding approach. Recently, there has been a significant number of debates and several lawsuits in the United States concerning the funding of public education. In recognition of this fact, it may now be advantageous to introduce into these debates an altogether different and truly equitable way to support education in this country.

Any effort to allow citizens to fulfill even part of their obligation regarding the right of a child to education by supporting private schools will encounter enormous resistance from those who have vested interests in perpetuating the existing state-run (so-called public) educational systems, such as teachers' unions and big businesses, including those in the text book, standardized testing, pharmaceutical, food, and computer industries. The best defense against such interests and powers, however, is to mount an aggressive offensive. One way to do this is to begin drafting and introducing model legislation that supports educational freedom and other models that recognize alternative funding choices in making the right of a child to education a financial reality. Considering the situation Waldorf education is facing today, there is nothing to lose by making such efforts. It is not being overly dramatic to say that the future course of human evolution depends on people taking such action in harmony with the ideals put forward by Steiner in relation to a threefold social organism.

CHAPTER 17

HOW CAN WE WORK TOGETHER? CHALLENGES OF INDIVIDUALISM AND THE NEED FOR TRUTHFULNESS

Before we consider specific ways to take practical steps to develop Waldorf education into the social force it was meant to be, there is another social aspect of Waldorf education that needs to be taken into consideration and that is the human relations within the school communities. On two different occasions Rudolf Steiner described that there are both social and antisocial forces working in every person and explained why the antisocial forces are becoming ever stronger as human evolution progresses.[91] He maintained that these antisocial forces, which are a by-product of the development of the human individuality, must be counterbalanced with ever stronger social forces, or else the antisocial element will gain the upper hand in human relations and in societal forms, including marriages, schools, businesses, and political organizations. In the past, human relations were more intuitive and part of the natural order of things, guided by the religious life or the ties of heredity. With the development of individuality, it is essential that we gain an understanding of the true nature of the human being and the forces that are at work within the soul. Then we can consciously work on the development of human relations in a way appropriate for modern times. This requires greater self-control and tolerance, intensified efforts to cultivate understanding of and interest in other people, and the development of morality out of one's inner life rather than through laws, dogma, or compulsory behavior modification mechanisms.

Steiner suggests that there are three practical ways to strengthen the social forces in the individual and social life in the face of ever-growing individualism. The first way is through the education of children. The strengthening of social forces in each child is an important aspect of the mission of Waldorf education. Through the curriculum the teachers in a Waldorf school strive to develop social understanding, sensitivity, and skills.

Social understanding is fostered, for instance, through the teaching of two foreign languages throughout the elementary school years, which enables young students to gain an understanding and appreciation of other cultures. *Social sensitivity* is enhanced by developing artistic ability and sensitivity in all course work including mathematics and science. *Social skills* are developed through drama, orchestra, community service, choral speech and singing, and group projects such as house building, cooking, gardening, and animal care.[92]

A second way to develop and strengthen social capacities, specifically in adults, is through inner exercises. One such exercise recommended by Steiner aims at strengthening our capacity to take objective interest in all people that we meet. He suggested looking back at the contributions that people have made in our lives when we were much younger, say ten or twelve years old. By consciously developing an appreciation for what people have contributed to our development in the past, we can gradually acquire the will forces to develop a real human interest in people who are a part of our lives now and for each new person who will cross our path in the future.

A third way to foster the social forces and to curb the antisocial forces is through establishing appropriate outer arrangements for cultural, political, and economic activities—in other words, by creating outer arrangements that are in harmony with the threefold nature of social life.

Consequently, as adults we have two possibilities of strengthening Waldorf communities socially. Firstly, we can develop an understanding of the social and antisocial forces that are a part of each one of us, and consciously and assiduously work to foster the social forces within us through inner exercises. Secondly, we can develop an understanding of the fundamental principles of a threefold social organism and work constructively to provide the proper social basis not only for the Waldorf school that we are connected to, but for *all* Waldorf schools and *all* children. Some ideas for the latter will be given in the following chapter.

Paradoxically, many people who are a part of Waldorf school communities observe that sometimes there appears to be even more antisocial behavior in them than in less idealistic endeavors. Why is this so? There are a number of contributing factors. One is the high degree of individual initiative needed in a Waldorf school. This applies not only to teachers but also to staff and legions of volunteers, including board members. A certain amount of egoism and the attendant antisocial forces are always present when individuals take initiative. Also, in a close-knit Waldorf school community, a large number of perspectives and strong opinions need to be taken into consideration before doing anything. This is a time-consuming process that outer circumstances often constrict. Another significant factor is that people in a close-knit community, consciously working on their inner development while outwardly striving with a mixture of self-interest and idealism, face otherwise dormant or deeply hidden aspects of their souls that unexpectedly come to the surface. If these unresolved, latent soul tendencies are not addressed in a right way, they can work into the community fabric through the personalities of its members and become magnified particularly through gossip and rumors. Hallway and parking-lot gossiping and rumor-making are infamous in their own right for their destructive nature.

And then, there is the challenging fact that a Waldorf school is trying to introduce an entirely unique approach to education, which requires new and evolving administration and governance forms.

There are many groupings or aspects of a school in which individual or group egoism can manifest in an unhealthy way. If there is not a common imagination or vision with which all participants can unite, the tendency to become more strongly attached to one facet of the school can and will take hold. This book is an effort to help Waldorf school supporters understand that the social goals of the Waldorf school movement are part of an overarching vision in which everyone in every school can unite.

The tendency toward separatism is an understandable and a natural consequence of the development of the human individuality. But it can develop into a social illness for the being of the school if conscious efforts are not made by the leadership and eventually by all Waldorf school supporters to go beyond their own personal attachment and standpoint to balance their individual perspectives with a sense for the whole school community and its underlying spiritual purpose.

Listed below are twelve potential fracture points that can occur *within* a Waldorf school community. Breakdowns can occur between:

Teachers
Teachers and parents
Teachers and administrative staff
Teachers and board of directors
Kindergarten, lower school, and high school
Full time and part time faculty/staff
Class teachers and specialty teachers
Anthroposophists and non-Anthroposophists
Members and non-members of the college of teachers
Teachers and students

Paid staff and volunteers

Mandated committees and everyone else

Rather than going into any detail explaining how divisiveness can manifest in the above groupings, we will focus on some aspects of human relations that affect all of these areas. This includes *human speech*. We each need to develop for ourselves a standard of conduct in relation to *right speech*. The typical verses expressing thoughts or ideals that are read aloud or referred to at the beginning of gatherings or meetings, but are not taken seriously, are in no way sufficient. Such spoken thoughts need to enter the soul life of every individual that takes initiative in a Waldorf school setting and become guidelines or standards for day-to-day conduct.

The ideals connected to right speech include how we speak to each other and about each other, in addition to developing a sense of when, and when not, to say certain things. In a close-knit community any form of gossip or rumor-mongering is social toxin. Right speech begins with developing a sense for absolute truthfulness. Rudolf Steiner required of students in the esoteric school within the Anthroposophical Society that above all else they make themselves responsible for feeling that they can seriously stand by every word they speak as being absolutely truthful. He maintained that untruthful statements, even when they come from good intentions, are destructive. Intentions are not what matter. It is objective truth that matters. This also needs to be a guiding principle for right speech in a Waldorf school community. This means that the leadership of the school, all those who take responsibility or initiative in any way, including the many parent volunteers, needs to exemplify this principle.

The quality of truthfulness is intimately connected to the quality of courage. It takes inner strength and courage to be truthful in what we say. In following the path of truthfulness we must steer our way through sentimentality or conventional political correctness, on the one hand, and tactlessness, rudeness, and lack of civility on the other. Critical comments should never be of the nature of a personal attack or directed at the individual worth of a person, but stay limited to their actions and behavior. Truthfulness and courage need to be cultivated and strengthened to a greater degree in a Waldorf community than what is normally deemed to be acceptable in the home or other community settings in order to achieve even basic civility and respect amongst the adults.

Withholding valid perspectives for fear of offending someone can rob a group of valuable insights that are necessary to make a fully informed decision. Even worse is the situation when a person withholds strongly held opinions on a particular issue in a group discussion or meeting but privately expresses them here and there afterward. This can have a particularly pernicious effect. Rudolf Steiner considered this type of behavior a terrible breach of rights amongst colleagues.[93]

In summary, antisocial tendencies in Waldorf school communities need to be overcome by developing counterbalancing soul virtues, particularly those of truthfulness and courage, working inwardly to strengthen the social forces that lie within us, and developing the right social forms within our schools so that they can assume their proper role in society as a whole.

CHAPTER 18

DEVELOPING THE WALDORF SCHOOL MOVEMENT INTO A POTENT SOCIAL FORCE

We will now present suggestions for certain types of initiatives that would need to take place in order for Waldorf education to thrive in the twenty-first century. It is essential that these proposed initiatives are wedded to a well-articulated vision or imagination of *both* the pedagogical and social missions of Waldorf education. These suggestions are not meant to be viewed as the only possibilities, nor does the implementation of any one of them guarantee success; rather they are meant to point in the direction we need to work to activate and guide our forces of will.

1. Create the twenty-first century version of the World School Association that Rudolf Steiner tried to launch during his lifetime. Such an organization could have an international character with affiliates around the world, including developing countries. For our purposes here, let us call such an initiative founded in the United States, *Independent Education in the Americas (IEA)*. An endeavor of this type could take up the following kinds of activities:

- Develop a world-wide mailing list of individuals and organizations supportive of educational freedom
- Articulate and promote the idea of educational freedom both within the Waldorf school movement and for the public through conferences, workshops, and a monthly or quarterly periodical

- Raise funds on a broad basis on behalf of Waldorf education
- Help to develop model educational projects that will show what can be achieved when educators and schools work out of freedom
- Use such model schools as case studies for fundraising efforts
- Monitor state, provincial, and federal legislation and its impact on independent education
- Draft model legislation to uphold the principle of freedom of choice for parents and self-administration for schools and to introduce alternative funding mechanisms for all private education such as the VASE approach previously mentioned

2. Revamp Waldorf teacher training institutes and programs. Teacher training programs focus mainly on basic Anthroposophy and pedagogical theory and technique. Teacher training institutes or programs need to give equal emphasis to three areas: Anthroposophy and pedagogy, administration, and the threefold nature of social life. Steiner wanted Waldorf teachers to be equally competent in both administration and teaching. Since self-administration is supposed to be an essential characteristic of a Waldorf school, it is a recipe for conflict and confusion if we do not prepare all teachers, at least to a basic degree, in the art and science of what Steiner calls the republican approach to administration mentioned in Chapter 5. National and international teachers' conferences could also place equal emphasis on pedagogy, administration, and threefold so teachers could continue to improve their understanding and skills in all three areas.

It is vital that teachers understand the *social* task or mission of Waldorf education and how it relates to the threefold nature of social life. This understanding is essential for people to rise above personal issues and conflicts and experience a unity of purpose within the Waldorf school movement. Just as we strive to develop social understanding, social skills, and social sensitivity in the students, so too the teacher trainings could do much more to help teachers themselves to progress in those areas.

3. *Educate Waldorf school communities about the social task of Waldorf education and its relation to the threefold nature of social life.* School parents are necessarily included here. This could be done in a variety of ways. On a national and international level, publications such as *Renewal,* which is published by the Association of Waldorf Schools in North America (AWSNA) and widely read in the Waldorf school movement, could begin to give equal editorial priority to the *social* task of Waldorf education as they do to the pedagogy. On the local level, schools could use their own brochures and newsletters. The local branches of the Anthroposophical Society could also play an instrumental role in arranging guest speakers and workshops on the social issues that a school is facing.

Too often parent education in a Waldorf school community is inadequate or focuses primarily on Waldorf teaching techniques. This often has the effect of enhancing parents' egoistic relation to Waldorf education and their criticism of the school, because they learn about the pedagogical ideals without the knowledge of the forces and the overarching social ideals it takes to achieve them. Much could be gained for the vitality and unity of a school community by focusing parent education on Anthroposophy and the threefold social organism and using this understanding in turn to illustrate the pedagogical aims.

4. *Articulate Waldorf educational goals, curriculum standards, and acceptable assessments for students and teachers in harmony with the principle of freedom in education.* While this suggestion may appear to contradict the principle of freedom, our age demands some type of explanation of how a school is educating children for practical life. If these things are done in the right spirit of honesty and in full recognition of what our social task is, we could remove a lot of confusion and concern on the part of parents and the public about Waldorf education. This would not only help with parent

appreciation and student retention in Waldorf schools, but it could be an essential component of a new vision of education for all schools. A newly-formed IEA (point 1) or AWSNA could coordinate the development of such an articulation of goals, standards, and acceptable assessments.

5. *Develop a national political organization with local chapters in each state or province that has a Waldorf school.* These chapters could be linked to and collaborate with an IEA-type of organization and work on a local level to educate the public about the importance of educational freedom as well as introducing favorable legislation and opposing unfavorable proposed laws.

6. *Think in terms of community rather than exclusively from an institutional perspective.* This is meant both geographically and by sector. On a local level, Waldorf schools need to consciously build connections with other groups and organizations. These connections could be economic, cultural, and/or political. Developing relations with the local community is an essential aspect of overcoming misconceptions and misunderstanding about the school and Waldorf education in general. A school could even forge new relations based on threefold principles. For example, when considering a purchase of land, rather than simply looking for a school site, a new or expanding school might think in terms of a developing a multifaceted community that includes housing, medical care, and farming, as well as retail, distribution, and manufacturing businesses. Those who appreciate Waldorf education are people who also often have an interest in affordable housing, sustainable agriculture, and socially responsible businesses. Thus, a Waldorf school can be a catalyst for communities being formed or transformed that would bring about a convergence of many innovative, alternative movements dealing with land, food, business, housing, and financial issues. Such community building efforts could open up whole new possibilities of economic, cultural, and legal support for Waldorf schools.

There may also be a possibility to develop links to the local community that would have direct economic impact through the creation of a local Waldorf school association similar to what Steiner and Molt created for the first Waldorf school. As previously described, it was a separate legal entity that took on the responsibility of fundraising for operations and capital needs. The goal of the organization was to relieve the faculty of the burden of balancing the budget and to let them focus on teaching. Such an entity may prove to be useful now and into the future. It could relieve schools from the pressure to seek wealthy people to be on school boards, people who may or may not understand self-administration or Waldorf education itself. Such people often get frustrated and leave disillusioned, or, if they stay for any period of time, try to introduce techniques that are effective in other settings but have a splintering effect in a Waldorf school. A separate entity that focuses on fundraising and development issues could provide such people with the opportunity to apply their good will, capacities, and resources on behalf of the school without subjecting them to administrative and decision making processes that are completely foreign to their personal experiences. A school could thus be much more liberal in whom they might include on such an independent board than they could be with selections for the board of the school itself. There are obviously certain pitfalls attached to creating such a separate fundraising organization, and any effort in this direction should proceed with *the school's* overall best interests in mind.

People connected to individual Waldorf schools also need to think in terms of educational communities in the broader sense: the Waldorf school movement, other independent schools, private schools, and education in general. Participation in all of these educational venues can provide support and opportunities for a greater understanding of Waldorf education and it social ideals.

These are a few suggestions of how people could begin in a practical way to implement the ideals that are at the heart of Waldorf education.

꩜

CHAPTER 19

PARADOXES, MISCONCEPTIONS, AND FALSE
STATEMENTS ABOUT WALDORF EDUCATION

A basic principle of the Association for the Threefolding of the Social Organism is to work toward an independent school system, making it free of the State so that the State does not even supervise the schools.
> – Rudolf Steiner *The Tasks of Schools and the Threefold Social Organism*, Stuttgart, Germany, June 1919[94]

If you do not have the courage to strive for the liberation of schools from the state, the whole Waldorf School Movement is of no avail.
> – Rudolf Steiner *The First University Course*, Dornach, Switzerland, October 1920[95]

Our education concerns itself with the methods of teaching and is essentially a new way and art of education, so every teacher can bring it into his work, in whatever kind of school he happens to be. . . . Our task is . . . to give indications of a way of teaching arising out of our anthroposophical knowledge of man.
> – Rudolf Steiner *The Roots of Education*, Bern, Switzerland, April 1924[96]

From the outset we were never interested in principles of educational method which might later on be somehow incorporated in a legalized educational system. What did interest us was reality, absolute true reality.
> – Rudolf Steiner *Human Values in Education*, Arheim, Holland, July 1924[97]

We will now show that a number of statements or opinions being circulated about what Rudolf Steiner said, intended, or did regarding the first Waldorf school have no basis in reality or have no correlation to circumstances now. These untruths introduce confusion, divert the attention from fundamental social tasks, and undermine the possibility of developing a strategy for advancing independent Waldorf education worldwide.

But first, let us address the question of what Rudolf Steiner meant by Waldorf *teaching methods* when he said, "Our education concerns itself with the methods of teaching and is essentially a new way and art of education, so every teacher can bring it into his work, in whatever kind of school he happens to be. . . . Our task is . . . to give indications of a way of teaching arising out of our anthroposophical knowledge of man." This may create a paradox in some people's minds because it appears to contradict the thoughts in the other quotations, which emphasize the necessity to separate education from the State.

In the lecture cycle in Bern, Switzerland, from which the quotation was taken regarding methods of teaching, and in a similar cycle, *Essentials of Education,*[98] given a few days prior in Stuttgart, Germany, Steiner is quite clear that Waldorf schools do not teach Anthroposophy, but rather Anthroposophy is the source and basis of the *teaching methods.* As he describes it, Waldorf methods flow out of Anthroposophy and the anthroposophical understanding of the human being. In the vast amount of material on Waldorf methods, it becomes evident that the art of teaching goes beyond mere outer techniques to include: cultivating a knowledge of body, soul, and spirit in relation to the human being; understanding the spiritual forces that a child brings to earth from pre-earthly life; understanding the necessity of the moral development of the teacher; developing a religious mood of soul out of which a person teaches; meditating on the children who are being taught; and viewing teaching as a priestly profession. These are all part of the Waldorf teaching methods as Steiner intended them to be.

With this in mind, let us now consider the apparent inconsistency and contradiction of the statement made by Steiner in Bern, Switzerland, in relation to the adjoining statements and others quoted throughout this book. Why, and in what context, did he say that Waldorf methods can be applied in any type of school one might be teaching in, if one of the social tasks of Waldorf education is to help liberate education from state control and create an independent school movement? First of all, it is important to note that it was only in Switzerland on certain occasions that Steiner spoke in this way. He was of the opinion that the sense for democracy at that time was different in Switzerland than in the rest of Europe. Accordingly, it was not possible for the Swiss to even consider the possibility of independent schools competing with State schools. Steiner therefore maintained that the only way to develop an independent Waldorf school movement in Switzerland was to introduce and establish independent Waldorf schools *as model schools* that could demonstrate a new "way of teaching arising out of our anthroposophical knowledge of man" for the benefit of all schools. Steiner's main goal was not to create State-run Waldorf schools but to create a conceptual basis and justification for establishing independent schools in Switzerland.[99]

There is no correlation between the situation that existed in Switzerland during Steiner's time and the situation of private education in the United States now. Approximately eleven percent of school-age children attend private schools in the United States. There is no need to position Waldorf schools as model schools in order to justify their existence. Even so, such statements by Steiner are now being used to rationalize efforts to incorporate Waldorf methods within the state system through public charter and magnet schools.

Let us now consider a number of recently circulated false ideas and erroneous facts that undermine any understanding of the relation of the first Waldorf school to the threefolding of society and educational freedom.

The first Waldorf school was publicly (government) funded.[100]

For anyone who has studied the material available about the early years of the Waldorf School under Steiner's direction and its relation to the movement for educational freedom and the threefolding of social life, the idea that the school was subsidized by the State is not within the realm of possibility. Irrefutable facts presented here demonstrate the falseness of such an idea, including the quoted words of F. Hartlieb, school inspector from the state of Würtemberg, when he stated in 1926 that the school was "not supported financially either by the State or by the town of Stuttgart, but is dependent entirely upon its own resources."[101]

Rudolf Steiner intended the first Waldorf school to be a "public," meaning state or government school.[102]

Again, an objective study of Steiner's and Molt's intentions and their deeds in relation to the first Waldorf school shows that this thought is not true. The source of this erroneous idea is a mistranslation from the German of certain passages in "The Pedagogical Basis of the Waldorf School," an essay that appeared in the periodical *The Threefold Social Order.* The key mistranslated sentence reads: "It is now planned that the Waldorf School will be a public school." The word "public" is a translation of the word *Volksschule.* The correct translation of *Volksschule* in this essay is *primary* or *elementary school,* meaning a school for children up to the age of 14, not a public school. This same essay also appears in the book *The Renewal of the Social Organism,* published by the Anthroposophic Press, and the word *Volksschule* is correctly translated there as "primary" school, not "public school."[103] From the context of the essay it is obvious *Volksschule* can only mean a primary or elementary school, for the whole essay is a description of pedagogical methods used with students up to the age of 14 years, and the essay itself is part of a series of essays on the threefold social organism, which explain why education and cultural life must be completely disassociated from the State and industry.[104]

Rudolf Steiner's vision for education, including Waldorf schools, was that they would exist within the State educational system, which would provide for the education but leave the educating to the teachers.[105]

It is unambiguous in Rudolf Steiner's writings and lectures on the threefold social organism that the State should no longer supervise, inspect, provide the facilities for, or fund education. The State's relation to education would be limited to such things as upholding safety regulations, contracts, the right of a child to an education, and the application of civil rights.

A passage in Steiner's book *Toward Social Renewal* may be the source of this mistaken idea. It reads: "Human culture has matured toward freedom within the framework of the State, but it cannot exercise this freedom without complete autonomy of action." But this statement is preceded and followed by thoughts which make it clear Steiner was not suggesting that complete autonomy for education can ever be found within the framework of the State: "For a new era in human relations to emerge, it was necessary that the circles which controlled education and culture be relieved of this function and that it be transferred to the political state. However, to persist in this arrangement is a grave social error . . . the nature which spiritual life has assumed requires that it constitute a fully autonomous member of the social organism."[106]

In a discussion after a lecture to young *public school* teachers in Germany, Rudolf Steiner made the following remark: "Someone also mentioned that it does not matter whether the person charged with developing thinking, feeling, and willing in a child does so within or outside the structure of the State. In spite of the fact that this question came up twice, I really cannot understand it. The important thing is that we not rob teachers of their strength of personality by cramming them into the confines of government regulations. You need only consider what it would mean if what entered the child's head did not come out of the free work of the teacher, but instead arose through regulations, curricula, and goals determined by the state."[107]

Steiner never suggested that it was possible to create a free space for education under the auspices and with the support of the State. Rather he declared that education needs to be removed from the State altogether.

Rudolf Steiner made a deal with the State in which he agreed that the students would and should be tested in grades 3, 6, and 8.[108]

As mentioned in Chapter 2, one of the three compromises that Rudolf Steiner made with government authorities was that the students would achieve learning goals equivalent to the local public school by the end of the third, sixth, and eighth grades. The fact that Steiner was willing to accept these compromises is often used to overcome present day concerns that Waldorf-inspired public schools need to submit to more and more state testing and curriculum standards. To what degree this compromise actually meant that the children were subjected to state tests, and to what degree Steiner approved of state testing, is revealed in the following passages. These are taken from notes of the conferences he had with teachers in the first school. The first series of excerpts is from a teachers' conference in April 1922, the third year of the Waldorf School.

"In the most important subjects we must bring the children to the point where they can pass exams."[109] Out of context this statement is ambiguous as to whether the students would actually take any kind of exam.

For further clarification, we continue. "We could give them supplementary reports saying that the pupil has reached [grade] 6 or [grade] 3 standard in such and such a subject in the following way. We shall not use marks. We will put it in a few reasonable words. This applies to [grades] 3, 6, 8, and 12. We have committed ourselves to do this. This special report must be given for [grade]

8." Steiner is suggesting that a special report written in the manner of a typical Waldorf report—a written summary of the abilities of the student by his or her teacher—is sufficient and even preferable to any type of letter or numerical grade. There is no indication that students had to be tested in any special way by the school, let alone by the state, to demonstrate their academic ability to fulfill the obligations of the compromise.

Continuing on: "If the children are not leaving, it is not necessary. We write them for those who need them. In the higher classes they only need them as leaving reports." Steiner's interpretation of his agreement with the State was that only those students who were going to leave the Waldorf School, which initially had only eight grades, needed a special report describing their academic achievements. It is apparent that Steiner did not want the students tested or evaluated in any special way other than what the teachers would prepare as an extra written report addressing their academic abilities in certain subjects.

Perhaps a better indication of what Steiner thought about at least one of the State tests of his day can be understood from the following statements by him in the fourth year of the School regarding the *Arbitur*, which is a series of required exams for twelfth grade students who want to go on to university.

Our chief worry is that in our top class we are, sad to say, actually being forced to deny our Waldorf School principles, for we cannot apply a curriculum that accords with them. We shall simply have to say that in the final year we shall have to teach all the subjects taught in local secondary schools, and do them the way they do them. In fact, I am already dreading the last half of the year when we shall have to stop everything else and concentrate entirely on the exam subjects. For one can scarcely imagine any other way of getting the pupils through the exams. It is a real worry.[110]

Obviously, Steiner was no enthusiastic supporter of state testing. It is interesting to note how the whole matter of the *Arbitur* was resolved during Steiner's time. The faculty, partly at the request of the students, decided to keep the Waldorf curriculum intact during the four years of high school, and as a compromise they offered a special exam preparation course separately in a thirtieth year.

CHAPTER 20

CONCLUDING THOUGHTS

Teachers and parents of Waldorf-inspired public schools may argue that these charter and magnet schools are enabling many children to receive the benefits of Waldorf education now who otherwise could not have it, and that these efforts have proven that Waldorf education can exist in the public school system without excessive restrictions for the teachers and students. It is completely understandable that frustrated and disheartened public school teachers and administrators who sincerely care about the children they are teaching are delighted to learn about Waldorf education and the possibility of employing Waldorf techniques in the public schools. The growing charter school movement in the United States has increased the possibility of doing so. And it is equally comprehensible why such people would think that anyone who appreciates Waldorf education and would say anything that might deprive them of its benefits is being a rigid idealist who is insensitive to the needs of economically disadvantaged families. It can also be acknowledged that the tuition being charged by independent Waldorf schools is far beyond the financial reach of what many parents can afford who want their children to attend Waldorf schools, and that there is growing frustration and resentment by many people because of this fact. All this can be fully acknowledged. Yet, it is the premise of this book, its reason for being, that true education in the twenty-first century can only occur in freedom and that it is the task of the Waldorf school movement to work unambiguously and with firm resolve to uphold educational freedom and the right of a child to an education in keeping with the ideals of a threefold social organism. The perspectives in this work arise from a concern for the present and future generations *of all children*. The intention is to present thoughts and ideals with which all individuals truly concerned about the education of children can unite, whatever one's position in life may be.

Even if there are situations here and there in the government-run education system where students are enjoying benefits from Waldorf techniques, and in the opinion of some there is no significant intrusion by the State at this time, such apparent freedom of action helps to justify and perpetuate the very government-controlled educational system that should be replaced by an independent cultural life and independent schools. Nor can this apparent freedom last in the long run. As already explained, we are only at the beginning stages of the implementation of national standards and testing now being mandated, and this includes charter schools. An equally important consideration for those concerned with the survival of independent Waldorf schools is the reality that all such efforts to incorporate Waldorf methods into public education draw attention, creative forces, money, teachers, and families away from Waldorf education's social mission on behalf of all children.

Waldorf-inspired public schools and independent Waldorf schools are, as institutions, competing entities that are in principle opposed to each other, despite the personal connections that exist between individuals working in each arena. If Waldorf-inspired public schools continue to grow in recognition and number, and people do not perceive any real difference between them and independent schools, then increasingly there will be no motive to pay private school tuition when the seemingly equivalent education can be obtained, apparently free of charge, at a Waldorf-inspired public school. Alternatively, if independent schools succeed in obtaining broad-based funding so that they are accessible to families of all economic backgrounds, then there is no significant reason to start or attend a Waldorf-inspired public school. Simply put, it all comes down to money.

Consider also how detrimental the following attitudes and actions of various Waldorf-inspired public schools advocates are for the very existence of independent Waldorf education:

- Portraying Waldorf inspired charter and magnet schools in a way that suggests there is no appreciable difference between them and independent Waldorf schools
- Reinterpreting the history of the first Waldorf School to justify charter school efforts
- Starting charter schools near independent schools and drawing families away from independent schools
- Encouraging independent schools to convert to being charter schools
- Encouraging independent school teachers to leave their schools and teach in Waldorf-inspired public schools
- Not revealing honestly and truthfully the degree to which compromises are being made in Waldorf-inspired public schools
- Suggesting that Waldorf-inspired public schools are teaching a more deserving population of students
- Stating that they are promoting the ideals of educational freedom and a threefold social organism through their support of Waldorf-inspired public schools
- Separating Waldorf education methods from Anthroposophy, the ideals of a threefold social organism, and Rudolf Steiner in teacher training institutes
- Dismissing or ignoring the fact the Waldorf-inspired public schools are the single greatest source of attacks on Anthroposophy and Rudolf Steiner in the United States, and

that they are drawing Anthroposophy and Waldorf education into the political arena and the court system

Some people quite rightly may observe that some independent schools are also distancing themselves from Anthroposophy and Rudolf Steiner and that they never had any conscious relation to the social mission as described in this book. The purpose of this work is to counteract such tendencies and to sound a wake-up call on behalf of the true pedagogical and social mission of Waldorf education.

If the independent Waldorf school movement had understood and seriously taken up its social task in response to the legitimate yearning of all true supporters of Waldorf education that it should be available to all children, the whole debate and controversy about Waldorf-inspired public schools would not have arisen in the first place—or not to the same degree—for there would have been significant and wide-spread efforts to make independent Waldorf schools accessible to families of all economic backgrounds. In the early 1990s, when independent Waldorf schools were becoming more and more expensive and financially out of reach for most families with no seeming recourse, the enticing possibility of creating an inner city Waldorf-inspired public school arose in Milwaukee, Wisconsin. In response, numerous experienced teachers from the independent Waldorf schools served as mentors for the project. Before any kind of review or evaluation was done, other Waldorf-inspired schools quickly emerged. Since then, numerous Waldorf teachers have left independent schools to work for new Waldorf-inspired public schools and help in the training of other teachers for such schools. The Waldorf-inspired public school movement owes its birth and continued existence to the knowledge and experience of former and current teachers in the independent Waldorf school movement.[111] From this viewpoint, Waldorf-inspired public schools are a self-created challenge by the independent school movement and a stark manifestation of its own inherent weakness and failing to live up to its social mission.

This characterization is not meant to denigrate individuals who choose to work for, enroll their children at, or help Waldorf-inspired public schools. The only reason for mentioning Waldorf-inspired public schools in this book is to bring to consciousness their relation to and their effect upon independent Waldorf schools. This work in meant to encourage all supporters of Waldorf education to gain an understanding of the ideals of the threefold nature of social life and the social mission of Waldorf education from the perspective of Anthroposophy, and to assess accordingly the long-term effects of their previous and current actions.

One may question why the perspectives and recommendations for the future of Waldorf education given here do not seem to take into consideration the experiences and circumstances of other countries, particularly those in Europe where the government subsidizes private schools. For some people, the European situation proves that independent schools can be funded by the government without suffering undue harm. The fact that several countries in Europe fund the operational and / or capital needs of Waldorf schools is often used to counter any concerns voiced about government intrusion if and when independent schools were to be funded by the government in the United States. However, it is important to recognize that most European countries, although perhaps proceeding in a less systematic way, are headed precisely in the same direction as the United States regarding national goals, standards, and assessments.[112] Those who positively view Waldorf-inspired public schools in the United States and government-funded independent Waldorf schools in Europe should consider the following thought by Rudolf Steiner: "Under certain conditions something can be made to fade out by treating it favorably for a while, thus gaining power over it. This can then make it easy to engulf it."[113] By enjoying the tax-derived government funding now and not working to develop broad-based financial support directly out of economic life in harmony with *both* educational freedom and the right of a child to an education, we are in fact setting ourselves up to be engulfed by the State and big business.

This book is written from the perspective of a person living in the United States of America at the beginning of the twenty-first century. Inevitably, place and time color every word herein. It is a time when United States economic, political, and military interests dominate the world. As we have pointed out, they also have a predominating influence on domestic concerns, particularly the field of education. These self-serving interests use education to perpetuate their existence by inculcating self-interested behavior, materialism, nationalism, and intellectualism into the rising generations.

These facts make it imperative that here and now in the United States of America creative spiritual forces of renewal flow from an autonomous educational system and cultural life into government and business. This is essential in order to counter-balance and turn to good the current unbridled economic, political, and military forces spreading throughout the world from the United States.

Based on a spiritual understanding of the human being and social life, Waldorf education was and is meant to be an instrumental force in freeing and renewing education and cultural life. To this end, this book encourages collaborative action on the part of as many people as possible to create the conditions that will enable Waldorf schools—and eventually all schools—to be:

- **Independent** with educators free to teach according to the unique needs of each and every child,
- **Privately funded** to the degree that teachers can earn a decent living and students can have proper facilities, and
- **Accessible to all** families regardless of their economic, cultural, or racial backgrounds.

There is no more important social endeavor at this time.

&&&

RUDOLF STEINER AS WORLD HUMANITARIAN AND SOCIAL REFORMER

Rudolf Steiner (1861–1925) was born in Central Europe in what is now Croatia. Early in his life he became aware of the spiritual world, which was not perceptible to other people around him and, therefore, was not something that he could talk about with them. As a young student, he worked assiduously to make a bridge between the spiritual reality that he could experience and the world accessible to the normal senses. Steiner worked throughout his whole life applying spiritual knowledge to practical life by combining his investigations of the supersensible with his knowledge of the various modern sciences both theoretical and applied.

Steiner wrote over forty books and gave approximately six thousand lectures covering a wide variety of fields including science, art, religion, education, medicine, architecture, economics, politics, philosophy, and inner development. He avoided defining or characterizing anything in a narrow or limited way, preferring to approach subjects from a broad and multifaceted perspective that included the spiritual basis of humanity and nature. This all-encompassing view can present challenges to those who approach the study of his works in a superficial manner.

Failure to accompany Steiner in thought through a range of perspectives on a subject can result, first of all, in a one-sided viewpoint, which, in turn, can foster dogmatism in the student if he or she latches onto certain statements to reinforce prejudices. In addition, it can leave the reader with a lack of appreciation for Steiner as a researcher and scientist.

Because of the universal nature of his works, people of the most divergent and even opposing political, economic, philosophical, and scientific viewpoints have used Steiner to support their positions. A variation or extension of this problem occurs when researchers look to Steiner to vindicate their previously held opinions and then, duly armed with Steiner quotations, evangelize their own beliefs to the world in an intolerant fashion. This is antithetical to the objective, rigorous research in which Steiner engaged himself . The failure to recognize Steiner's all-encompassing approach, which goes beyond merely considering the physical world, has made Steiner subject to personal attacks and being accused of certain prejudices and moral failures, including racism, nationalism, and anti-Semitism. Space does not allow an in-depth discussion on specific accusations here.[114] For now this appendix is offered as one important perspective on the issue, how Steiner's ideas on the threefold nature of social life address the three root causes of social unrest and upheaval in the world already mentioned in the Introduction: economic exploitation of people[115] and the environment based on self-interested behavior; political oppression by powerful interest groups; and cultural intolerance, including racism, nationalism, and religious and scientific fanaticism.

Steiner had the greatest possible respect for and confidence in the abiding human spirit manifest in every human being. He recognized the necessity for individual freedom in all personal and cultural matters. He maintained that "live and let live" is the governing principle for cultural life, which includes religion, scientific views, and educational choices, *as long as* one's actions do not harm or exploit others. Not adhering to this principle has resulted in havoc being wrought in the world through fundamentalism, fanaticism, and ideological militarism and terrorism. Instead, it is the divine principle of individual freedom that must prevail now, regardless of a person's race, nationality, or beliefs.

Steiner's critics often focus on what he said about the origin and past influences of one or another racial, national, religious, or other group and how they affect the present. An objective study of his universal perspective shows that he analyzed with equal discernment the characteristics of various groups of people and that he called all groups to task about their failures, inadequacies, and one-sided tendencies. Furthermore, critics often dismiss or minimize the importance of Steiner's views on the present and future evolution of humanity. From this anthroposophical perspective of the appropriate path of evolution, all of humanity is evolving toward greater and greater individuality and freedom. Consequently, Steiner maintained that we are at the point in human evolution when differences according to groupings such as gender, race, culture, caste, or nation should become, *and are in reality, meaningless* insofar as determining the worth or significance of a human being.[116] Steiner maintained that regardless of the role or importance these groupings had in the past, they are no longer of any significance now in relation to what he called the *universal human*: the spiritual, immortal essence of every person.[117] According to Steiner this is a key concept that can provide the basis for overcoming outer differences in the world.

The concept of the universal human can lead us to an appropriate understanding of the role, dynamics, and basis for the political State. When, through Anthroposophy, we correctly understand the meaning and importance of the ancient principle "equal in the eyes of God," it will become possible in modern times to fully realize genuine equality in earthly human relations. Only when each person becomes equal in the eyes of the other within the political state, can human relations become truly civil. Recognition of the universal human is the divine basis for the principle of equality and for a truly democratic political state. Through understanding the principle of equality and what one might call its descent from the heavens, and through implementation of true democracy in a threefold society, we can also understand the proper limits of State action. Steiner asserted that because of our failure to understand

and live by the principle of equality we give the State powers it should not have.

Recognition of the universal human element can also provide a new basis for economic life, which is presently dominated by self-interested behavior. Steiner maintained that through recognition of the universal human, we can achieve an understanding of the spiritual unity of all humanity and gain the possibility of going beyond self-interested behavior through the power of love. Steiner elaborated an economic approach or theory called associative economics, as mentioned in Chapter 1. He was one of the first economists to recognize the interdependent, global nature of economic life, the negative effects of accelerated growth, and the necessity of replacing the impersonal market based on self-interested behavior with an associative economy based on fellowship and conscious relations between the producers, consumers, and distributors who are active in a given area.

From these brief indications about Steiner's social strivings in connection to the threefold nature of social life, one can gain a sense of his vast and positive contribution to humanity and how society could be structured to enable people of all cultural, racial, and economic backgrounds to live together in peace, respect, prosperity, and good will.

APPENDIX (B)

AN INVITATION TO THE READERS OF THIS BOOK

It is my hope that this book will help stimulate a world-wide interest in educational freedom and new ways to support independent schools. Anyone who has found this book of value is invited to contact me with comments and suggestions for improving future editions. Not only would I like to hear from people connected to private education but also from parents, teachers, administrators, and students who are a part of the public education system who are willing to describe how the government reform programs described here are affecting them professionally and personally.

I am joining a number of like-minded colleagues to work in practical ways to implement suggestions that are given in Chapter 18, and we would also like to collaborate with others who want to or are already engaged in similar efforts.

Please send your comments and contact information, including email and postal addresses, to: Gary Lamb, PO Box 329, Philmont, NY 12565 USA.

Footnotes:

1 The term "Waldorf-inspired" public schools refers to both public charter schools and public magnet schools. Public magnet schools typically receive financial aid to desegregate a student population; they often use a specialized curriculum to attract students. Public charter schools can be set up by government-approved groups or individuals under a contract or charter to operate as a public school.

The January 1996 "Position Statement" of the Association of Waldorf Schools in North America (AWSNA) states: "Because of the autonomous nature of an independent Waldorf school, it is not possible, at this point in time with the current legal and political constraints in the U.S. on educational freedom, to have a Waldorf school in the public sector. Waldorf is a trademark name in the United States and is reserved for a school that is free and independent of government controls. Therefore, a school in the U.S. using Waldorf methods in the public sector cannot be named "Waldorf." A subtitle under the name of the school could, however, include the wording 'Waldorf-inspired'."

2 Opponents to so-called Waldorf-inspired public schools have also challenged them in courts claiming that Anthroposophy is a religion and that they violate the so-called separation of church and state doctrine.

3 Steiner, Rudolf. *The Renewal of the Social Organism*, Spring Valley, NY: Anthroposophic Press, 1985, p. 75. A collection of articles written in 1919 and 1920. From the essay "The Threefold Social Order and Educational Freedom."

4 No distinction is made here between direct and representational democracy.

5 For further information on threefold ideas, see: *Towards Social Renewal* and *Renewal of the Social Organism* by Rudolf Steiner available from Steiner Books, Herndon, VA 20172.

6 *The Coming Day in Germany* (described in a later chapter) and the Futurum enterprise in Switzerland were holding companies established to provide economic support for cultural activities. The World School Association is described in Chapter 4. The Anthroposophical Society, based in Dornach, Switzerland, is a world-wide organization, initially formed in 1913 to foster the anthroposophical worldview; it was re-founded in 1923. In 1922, Rudolf Steiner gave a lecture cycle on world economy in which he outlined a new economic science based

on the principle of association, which would replace the market system.

7 Permaculture is a system of perennial agriculture that emphasizes the use of natural resources and local ecosystems.

8 See "Meeting the Challenge of Globalization" and "Civil Society: Remedy or Distraction" by Gary Lamb, *The Threefold Review*, Philmont, NY: Summer / Fall 1999, No. 18.

9 Steiner, Rudolf. *Rudolf Steiner in the Waldorf School: Lectures and Addresses to Children, Parents, and Teachers, 1919–1924,* Hudson, NY: Anthroposophic Press, 1996, p. 158. From an address at the second official members' meeting of the Independent Waldorf School Association, June 20, 1922.

10 Steiner, Rudolf. *The Spirit of the Waldorf School,* Hudson, NY: Anthroposophic Press, 1995, p. 7.

11 Available from Steiner Books, Herndon, VA 20172.

12 Molt, Emil. *Emil Molt and the Beginnings of the Waldorf School Movement: Sketches from an Autobiography,* Edinburgh: Floris Books, 1991, p. 137.

13 Steiner, Rudolf. *Education as a Force for Social Change*, Hudson, NY: Anthroposophic Press, 1997, p. 105.

14 Molt, Emil. *Emil Molt and the Beginnings of the Waldorf School Movement: Sketches from an Autobiography,* Edinburgh: Floris Books, 1991, p. 137.

15 Molt, Emil. *Emil Molt and the Beginnings of the Waldorf School Movement: Sketches from an Autobiography,* Edinburgh: Floris Books, 1991, p. 142.

16 Steiner, Rudolf. *Faculty Meetings with Rudolf Steiner, 1919–1922, Volume 1,* Hudson, NY: Anthroposophic Press, 1998, p. xvii.

17 Steiner, Rudolf. *Conferences with the Teachers of the Waldorf School in Stuttgart, 1919 to 1920, Volume One,* Forest Row, UK: Steiner Schools Fellowship Publications, 1986, p. 12. From the introduction by Erich Gabert. This informative observation is left out of the more recent edition of the teachers conferences: *Faculty Meetings with Rudolf Steiner.*

18 Hartlieb, F. *The Free Waldorf School at Stuttgart*, London: Anthroposophical Publishing Company, 1928, p. 6.

19 Steiner, Rudolf. *Conferences with the Teachers of the Waldorf School in Stuttgart, 1919 to 1920, Volume One*, Forest Row, UK: Steiner Schools Fellowship Publications, 1986, p. 34. The address by Rudolf Steiner given on August 20, 1919, from which this extract was taken, is omitted from the more recent edition of the teachers' conferences *Faculty Meetings with Rudolf Steiner*. It does appear, however, in *The Foundations of Human Experience* (1996) published by the Anthroposophic Press.

20 Steiner, Rudolf. *Faculty Meetings with Rudolf Steiner, 1919–1922, Volume I*, Hudson, NY: Anthroposophic Press, 1998, p. 170. September 21, 1920, conference.

21 In response to a direct question put to him by Rudolf Steiner during a conference, Emil Molt admitted to the teachers the degree to which he personally financed the School and that he, not the Waldorf Astoria firm, actually owned the school.

"Dr. Steiner: 'I have the feeling that from the financial point of view as well, Herr Molt has founded the whole Waldorf School as a private individual. The Waldorf Astoria Factory has certainly added its contribution to what Herr Molt has done personally, but—although this may not be opportune—the truth is that Herr Molt's cash box represents most of it, doesn't it?'

Herr Molt: 'It is embarrassing to talk about it. The school that is registered as such is my private possession. The building costs were defrayed by me. The school pays no rent.' "

Steiner, Rudolf. *Conferences with the Teachers of the Waldorf School in Stuttgart, 1919–1920, Volume One*, Forest Row, UK: Steiner Schools Fellowship Publications, 1986, p. 107. July 29, 1920, conference.

22 Steiner, Rudolf. *Faculty Meetings with Rudolf Steiner, 1919–1922, Volume 1*, Hudson, NY: Anthroposopshic Press, 1998, p. xxi.

23 Steiner, Rudolf. *Faculty Meetings with Rudolf Steiner, 1919–1922, Volume 1*, Hudson, NY: Anthroposopshic Press, 1998, p. 146.

24 Steiner, Rudolf. *Conferences with the Teachers of the First Waldorf School in Stuttgart, 1919 to 1920, Volume One*, Forest Row, UK: Steiner Schools Fellowship Publications, 1986, p. 108.

25 Molt, Emil. *Emil Molt and the Beginnings of the Waldorf School Movement: Sketches from an Autobiography*, Edinburgh: Floris Books, 1991, pp. 148–150.

26 Steiner, Rudolf. *Faculty Meetings with Rudolf Steiner: 1919–1922, Volume 1*, Hudson, NY: Anthroposophic Press, 1998, pp. 131 and 135.

27 For more information on The Coming Day see: Houghton Budd, Christopher. *Rudolf Steiner: Economist*, Canterbury, England: New Economy Publications. Chapter titled "A Brief History of Der Kommenden Tag" by E. Leinhas.

28 Steiner, Rudolf. *Faculty Meetings with Rudolf Steiner, Volume 1, 1919–1922*, Hudson, NY: Anthroposophic Press, 1998, pp. 130, 131.

29 Steiner, Rudolf. *Education as an Art*, Blauvelt, NY: Rudolf Steiner Publications, 1970, p. 74. A public lecture given at The Hague, Holland, February 27, 1921, titled "The Science of Spirit, Education and Practical Life."

30 Steiner, Rudolf. *The Threefold Review*, Philmont, NY: The Margaret Fuller Corporation, Issue no. 2, 1989, p. 7. As quoted in the article "How Important Is it that Schools Be Independent Today?" by Helmut van Kügelgen. Steiner made this statement in Utrecht, February 24, 1921.

31 Steiner, Rudolf. *Faculty Meetings with Rudolf Steiner, 1919–1922, Volume I*, Hudson, NY: Anthroposophic Press, 1998. pp. 138 and 139. From a teachers' conference that took place on July 29, 1920.

32 Steiner, Rudolf. *The New Spirituality and the Christ Experience of the Twentieth Century*, London: Rudolf Steiner Press, 1988, p. 25. From a lecture given on October 17, 1920 in Dornach, Switzerland.

33 Steiner, Rudolf. *Soul Economy and Waldorf Education*, Spring Valley, NY: Anthroposophic Press, 1986, p. 318. Lectures and discussions given in Dornach, Switzerland, between December 23, 1921, and January 7, 1922. From a discussion on January 3, 1922.

34 Steiner, Rudolf. *Education as an Art*, Blauvelt, NY: Rudolf Steiner Publications, 1970, p. 74. A public lecture given in The Hague, Holland, February 27, 1921, titled "The Science of Spirit, Education and Practical Life."

35 Steiner, Rudolf. *The Threefold Review*, Philmont, NY: The Margaret Fuller Corporation, Issue no. 2, 1989, p. 4. As quoted in the article "How Important Is It that Schools Be Independent Today?" by Helmut van Kügelgen. Steiner made this statement in Dornach, Switzerland, October 1920.

36 Steiner, Rudolf. *Rudolf Steiner in the Waldorf School: Lectures and Addresses to Children, Parents, and Teachers, 1919–1924*, Hudson, NY, 1996: Anthroposophic Press, pp. 158–163. From an address at the second official members' meeting of the Independent Waldorf School Association, June 20, 1922.

37 Steiner, Rudolf. *Soul Economy and Waldorf Education*, Spring Valley, NY: Anthroposophic Press, 1986, p. 318. Lectures and discussions given in Dornach, Switzerland, between December 23, 1921, and January 7, 1922. From a discussion of January 3, 1922.

38 Steiner, Rudolf. *Towards Social Renewal*, London: Rudolf Steiner Press, 1977, p. 12.

39 Steiner, Rudolf. *The Social Future*, Spring Valley, NY: Anthroposophic Press, 1972, pp. 28–29. Public lectures given in Zurich, October 24–30, 1919.

40 Steiner, Rudolf. *The Renewal of the Social Organism*, Spring Valley, New York: Anthroposophic Press, 1985, p. 75 (articles published in 1919 and 1920). From "The Threefold Social Order and Educational Freedom."

41 Steiner, Rudolf. *The Spirit of the Waldorf School*, Hudson, New York: Anthroposophic Press, 1995, pp. 168 and 169. From a lecture given in Basel, Switzerland, "The Social Pedagogical Significance of Spiritual Science," November 25, 1919.

42 Steiner, Rudolf. *Waldorf Education and Anthroposophy*, Hudson, NY: Anthroposophic Press, pp. 51–52. From a lecture given in The Hague, "Education and Practical Life from the Perspective of Spiritual Science," February 27, 1921.

43 Steiner, Rudolf. *Conferences with the Teachers of the First Waldorf School in Stuttgart, 1919 to 1920, Volume One*, Forest Row, UK: Steiner Schools Fellowship Publications, 1986, p. 34.

44 Steiner, Rudolf. *Soul Economy and Waldorf Education,* Spring Valley, NY: The Anthroposophic Press, 1986, pp. 314–315. Lectures given in Dornach, Switzerland, December 23, 1921–January 7, 1922.

45 Steiner, Rudolf. *Towards Social Renewal,* London: Rudolf Steiner Press, 1977, pp. 11–12.

46 Steiner, Rudolf. "The Task of Schools and The Threefold Social Organism." In *The Threefold Review*, Philmont, NY: Margaret Fuller Corporation, Issue No. 20, Fall 2002, p. 31.

47 Steiner, Rudolf. *New Aspects of the Social Question,* London: Rudolf Steiner Publishing, (no publishing date), pp. 27 and 28. From a lecture given in Berlin, September, 15, 1919.

48 Steiner, Rudolf. *A Social Basis for Primary and Secondary Education,* Garden City, NY: Waldorf Institute, Adelphi University, 1975, p. 42. Lectures given in Stuttgart, May–June 1919.

49 Steiner, Rudolf. *Towards Social Renewal,* London: Rudolf Steiner Press, 1977, pp. 114–116.

50 The National Commission on Excellence in Education, *A Nation at Risk: the Imperative for Educational Reform,* Washington DC: U.S. Department of Education, 1983, pp. 5–7. It is important to note that the major economic concerns raised in the report have been historically proven to be insignificant, not worthy of throwing a whole nation into hysteria and initiating major legislation and allocating billions of dollars. Japan's and Korea's economies have taken significant downturns since this report was written, even with huge subsidies and a highly competitive education system on the part of Japan.

51 "One Nation, One Curriculum?" *Newsweek,* April 6, 1992, p. 60.

52 U.S. Department of Education. *The National Goals for Education,* Washington, DC: U.S. Department of Education, July, 1990.

53 "Educational Council Proposes National Standards for Students," Albany, NY: *Times Union*, December 18, 1991.

54 This statement is taken from the Business Roundtable website at www.businessroundtable.org/aboutus.

55 *Business Means Business about Education: A Synopsis of the Business Roundtable Companies Education Partnerships*, New York: The Business Roundtable, December 1989, p. 2.

56 *The Role of Business in Education Reform: Blueprint for Action,* New York: The Business Roundtable, April 1988.

57 *Business Means Business about Education: A Synopsis of the Business Roundtable Companies Education Partnerships,* New York: The Business Roundtable, December 1989, p.2.

58 *The Role of Business in Education Reform: Blueprint for Action,* New York: The Business Roundtable, April 1988.

59 *The Role of Business in Education Reform: Blueprint for Action,* New York: The Business Roundtable, April 1988.

60 *The Business Role in State Educational Reform,* New York: The Business Roundtable, 1990, p. 6.

61 *The Business Roundtable Participation Guide: A Primer for Business on Education,* New York: The Business Roundtable, April 1991, p. 40. Developed by the National Alliance of Business.

62 *Continuing the Commitment: Essential Components of a Successful Educational System: The Business Roundtable Education Public Policy Agenda,* New York: The Business Roundtable, May 1995, pp. 2 and 3.

63 *Continuing the Commitment: Essential Components of a Successful Educational System: The Business Roundtable Education Public Policy Agenda,* New York: The Business Roundtable, May 1995, p.7.

64 "One Nation, One Curriculum?": *Newsweek,* April 6, 1992, p. 59–60.

65 *Continuing the Commitment: Essential Components of a Successful Educational System: The Business Roundtable Education Public Policy Agenda,* New York: The Business Roundtable, May 1995, p. 8.

66 *Continuing the Commitment: Essential Components of a Successful Educational System: The Business Roundtable Education Public Policy Agenda,* New York: The Business Roundtable, May 1995, p. 12.

67 The Constitution assigns no power to the United States government regarding education. Education comes under the jurisdiction of Amendment X, which states: "The powers not delegated to the United States by the Constitution, nor prohibited by it to the States, are reserved to the States respectively, or to the people."

68 *No Turning Back,* Washington, DC: The Business Roundtable: June 1, 1999.

69 For an extensive analysis of *Goals 2000: Educate America Act,* see Milito, Ronald, "Goals 2000: What Have We Done with Our Freedom," Philmont, NY: *The Threefold Review,* Summer/Fall 1995, Issue no. 12.

70 The two additional goals are: "The nation's teaching force will have access to programs for the continued improvement of their professional skill and the opportunity to acquire the knowledge and skills needed to instruct and prepare all American students for the next century" and "Every school will promote partnerships that will increase parental involvement and participation in promoting the social, emotional and academic growth of children."

71 U. S. House of Representatives. *Goals 2000: Educate America Act,* Washington, DC: House of Representatives Conference Report, March 21, 1994, pp. 4–5.

72 See Lamb, Gary. "Collusion, Fraud, and Abdication of Power: The Legacy of *Goals 2000,*" Philmont, NY: *The Threefold Review,* Summer/Fall 1994, Issue No. 11, p. 20.

73 U. S. House of Representatives. *Goals 2000: Educate America Act,* Washington, DC: House of Representatives Conference Report, March 21, 1994, p. 16.

74 *The Threefold Review.* "1996 National Education Summit Policy Statement," Philmont, NY: *The Threefold Review,* Summer/Fall 1996, Issue no. 14, p. 6.

75 Achieve, Inc. "The 1999 National Education Summit," Washington, DC: Achieve, Inc., 1999, P.3.

76 1999 Summit Website. "Governors, CEO's & Educators Meet to Accelerate Improvement in US Schools: 1999 National Education Summit," Summit Website, www.summit99.org. Listed under Announcement/Releases.

77 "1999 National Education Summit," Washington, DC: Achieve, Inc., 1999, p. 10.

78 "1999 National Education Summit," Washington, DC: Achieve, Inc., 1999, p. 4.

79 "1999 National Education Summit," Washington, DC: Achieve, Inc., 1999, p. 4.

80 "1999 National Education Summit," Washington, DC: Achieve, Inc., 1999, p. 10.

81 See, for instance, the BRT press release of September 13, 2000, "New Survey Challenges Extent of Public School Backlash Against State Testing" in which the BRT sponsored its own opinion poll to counter media reports that a widespread backlash against standards-based testing was taking place.

82 "The 2001 National Education Summit," Washington, DC: Achieve Inc., 2001, p. 1.

83 "2001 National Education Summit," Washington, DC: Achieve Inc., 2001, p. 2.

84 "Executive Summary of the 'No Child Left Behind Act of 2001', " Washington, DC: The Business Roundtable, 2001, p. 1.

85 Vernier Software and Technology. "'No Child Left Behind' and You," Beaverton, OR: Vernier Software and Technology, 2003, p.1.

86 "'No Child Left' Behind Business Leaders Toolkit: Action Steps," Washington, DC: The Business Roundtable, 2001.

87 "Business Leader's Guide to Setting Academic Standards," Washington, DC: The Business Roundtable, June 1996, p. 2.

88 Steiner, Rudolf. As quoted by Hans-Werner Schroeder in "The End of the Century and Ahriman's Incarnation in the Following Millennium," Ann Arbor, MI: *Newsletter of the Anthroposophical Society in America*, Autumn, 1998, p. 3. Translated from German into English by Maria St. Goar from the lecture cycle *Gegenwärtiges und Vergangenes im Menschengeiste,* GA 167.

89 In the United States private schools or private education include both parochial and independent schools.

90 There may be some isolated cases which may appear to be exceptions to this view. For instance, in the state of Vermont certain school districts without a public high school pay the tuition for high school students who attend local private schools without undue restrictions. But if the federal reform efforts described here take effect as intended, even these types of exceptions will not long be available.

91 Steiner, Rudolf. *Social and Antisocial Forces in the Human Being*, Spring Valley, NY: Mercury Press, 1995.

92 See Strawe, Christoph. "Developing Social Skills, Social Understanding and Social Sensitivity in Rudolf Steiner Waldorf Schools," *Paideia*, Forest Row, England: Steiner Waldorf Schools Fellowship, April 1998, Number 16, pp. 31–44.

93 Steiner, Rudolf. *The Fundamental Social Demand of Our Time*, Harlemville, NY: Rudolf Steiner Library of the Anthroposophical Society in America. An undated manuscript of lecture three given on December 15, 1918.

94 Steiner, Rudolf. "The Tasks of Schools and the Threefold Social Organism," *The Threefold Review*, Philmont, NY: The Margaret Fuller Corporation, Issue no. 20, Fall 2002, p. 30. A lecture given in Stuttgart, Germany, June 19, 1919, to the Association of Young Teachers.

95 Steiner, Rudolf as quoted in "How Important Is it That Schools Be Independent Today?" by Helmut von Kügelgen in *The Threefold Review*, Issue no. 2, Winter 1989, p. 4. Originally published in *Erziehungskunst*, June 1964. The English translation by Lisa Monges first appeared in the Autumn 1980 issue of the *Journal for Anthroposophy*. Steiner made this statement to students at The First University Course given in Dornach, Switzerland, October 1920.

96 Steiner, Rudolf. *The Roots of Education*, London: Rudolf Steiner Press, 1968, p. 28. Five lectures given in Bern, Switzerland, April 13–17, 1924.

97 Steiner, Rudolf. *Human Values in Education*, London: Rudolf Steiner Press, pp. 22. Lectures given in Arheim, Holland, July 17-24, 1924.

98 Steiner, Rudolf, *The Essentials of Education*, Hudson, NY, 1997: Anthroposophic Press, 1971. Lectures given in April, 1924, in Stuttgart, Germany.

99 See Steiner, Rudolf. "Rudolf Steiner's Contribution during the Meeting of the Swiss School Association, 28 December 1923," *The Christmas Conference*, Hudson, NY: The Anthroposophic Press.

100 See Clouder, Christopher. "In Dialogue with the Worldly Powers: Waldorf Education in the European Union," *Renewal*, Fair Oaks, CA: Association of Waldorf Schools of North America, Spring/Summer 2003.

101 See reference number 18.

102 From an audio transcript of a 2004 workshop conducted by Merrill Badger at the (independent) Enchanted Desert Waldorf school in Tucson, AZ.

103 See Steiner, Rudolf. "The Pedagogical Basis of the Waldorf School," *The Renewal of the Social Organism*, Hudson, NY: Anthroposophic Press, 1985.

104 See Steiner, Rudolf. "The Threefold Social Order and Educational Freedom," *The Renewal of the Social Organism*, Hudson, NY: Anthroposophic Press, 1985.

105 See Rawson, Martyn. "What Is the Spirit of the School Trying to Tell Us?" *Paideia*, Forest Row, England: Steiner Waldorf Schools Fellowship, Issue No. 16, April 1998, p. 10.

106 Steiner, Rudolf. *Towards Social Renewal*, London: Rudolf Steiner Press, 1977, p. 12.

107 Steiner, Rudolf. "The Tasks of Schools and the Threefold Social Organism," *The Threefold Review*, Philmont, NY: The Margaret Fuller Corporation, Issue no. 20, Fall 2002, p. 32. A lecture given in Stuttgart, Germany, June 19, 1919, to The Association of Young Teachers.

108 From an audio transcript of a 2004 workshop conducted by Merrill Badger at the Enchanted Desert Waldorf School in Tucson, AZ.

109 Steiner, Rudolf. *Conferences with the Teachers of the Waldorf School in Stuttgart, 1921–1922, Volume Two*, Forest Row, UK: Steiner Schools Fellowship Publications, 1987, pp. 61–62. This conference was held at 4:30 pm, April 28, 1922.

110 Steiner, Rudolf. *Conferences with the Teachers of the Waldorf School in Stuttgart, 1923–1924, Volume Four*, Forest Row, UK: Steiner Schools Fellowship Publications, 1989, p. 15. This conference was held at 4:30 pm, April 25, 1923.

111 Taking everything into consideration one can see that Waldorf-inspired public schools are not simply competitors with independent Waldorf schools, they also have a parasitic relation to them. Spiritually-based cultural endeavors, including schools, cannot sustain themselves within the framework of the State. Sources of spiri-

tual renewal must come from individuals and organizations active outside the State's domain. This is why in the 1980s, when it was starkly clear that public education was in big trouble, politicians looked mainly, though mistakenly, to big business, not to public school educators for creative ideas. So too, the Waldorf-inspired public school movement of necessity needs to continually draw upon current and former teachers and administrators from the independent Waldorf school movement for its survival. This does not mean that people working under the jurisdiction of the state can't have a rich inner life and bring this to bear in the classroom. It means that as teachers their creative inspirations must ultimately serve the standards and goals of the state and big business.

112 See Lamb, Gary. "From Strings to Ropes: Education Reform in Britain," and "Dutch Education Update: More Outcomes-Based Education," *The Threefold Review*, Philmont, NY: The Margaret Fuller Corporation, Issue No. 9, Summer / Fall 1993.

There are places in Europe that have significant State testing already, which many people take for granted. However, the breadth and magnitude of educational standards and testing about to be implemented in the United States is greater than what presently prevails in Europe.

113 Steiner, Rudolf. *The Karma of Untruthfulness, Volume I*, London: Rudolf Steiner Press, p. 236. Thirteen lectures given in Dornach and Basel, Switzerland, in December 1916.

114 For some people this may be an inadequate response to specific statements made by Steiner. A more in-depth discussion is required to adequately address these types of concerns, a project that I look forward to engaging in sometime in the near future. For now this appendix is offered as one essential perspective on the issue.

115 See *Anthroposophy and the Social Question* by Rudolf Steiner, available from the Mercury Press, Chestnut Ridge, NY, for his perspective on economic exploitation.

116 Steiner developed this idea in a number of places, including Lecture 9 of the 1911 lecture cycle *The Influence of Spiritual Beings upon Man* and the lecture "Individuality and the Group Soul" (Munich, December 4, 1909) in the book *The Universal Human* published by the Anthroposophic Press.

117 See, for instance, the lecture "The Universal Human: The Unification of Humanity through the Christ Impulse" (Bern, Switzerland, January 9, 1916) in the book *The Universal Human* published by the Anthroposophic Press.